Praise for *The Money Chimp*

"If your intention is to build wealth and be financially free then your journey starts by investing in your own personal development and improving your financial literacy. *The Money Chimp* is a must-read for anyone who needs to learn how to manage their money especially 18-25s."

Steve Bolton
CEO, *Platinum Property Partners*

"This is the best book on managing money for 18-25s I have read. If you are 18-25 (or older) and you follow the steps in this book, you will be free of money worries for the rest of your life!"

Karen Sutton-Johal
Debt Advisor, *The 4 Money Mindsets*

"A must-read for anyone who wants to understand their relationship with money. Loads of smart tips and recommendations with lots of relevant examples and anecdotes. We all should take actionable steps by doing a comprehensive fact-find then creating a *Lifestyle Financial Plan*. After-all, life is not a rehearsal! Take *The Money Chimp* test."

Simon Jeffries
Founder/MD, *Asset Wealth Creation*

"This is a must-read for those who are serious about building wealth. You won't learn this information at school which is why 18-25s are the most susceptible to chronic debt. Filled with practical case studies, money management techniques and wealth generation ideas this book is a great tool for debt busting and helping you create the wealth you need to live your best life on purpose."

Sonia Brown MBE
Founder/Director, *National Black Women's Network*

"A wonderful book from the master of business coaches, Andrew Priestley. While it is not always possible to put wise heads on young shoulders, this book goes a long way towards achieving that. Financial literacy should be a central part of our education system and this book provides the knowledge and the strategy for all young people to develop financial street smarts."

Andrew Fuller
Clinical Psychologist/Family Therapist
Bestselling Author, Resilient Youth Australia

"We educate our children in maths and while there is growing awareness of the need to educate them in money management this is happening too slowly and doesn't help those who have already left school or a building up university debt. This book is a quick way to become financially skilled with practical solutions all presented in an easy read. It's targeted at young adults but I think it gives such good practical advice that you can put into action and benefit from whatever age you are."

Sonia Gill
Educator, Author, Founder/Director, *Heads Up (UK)*

"Andrew Priestley says that people tend to write some 'software' in their heads about money when they are kids and don't update the 'files' later in life. I believe him. The useful and practical tips in this well-researched and readable book may be just what the doctor ordered to update your files and re-order your mindset, beliefs and perceptions about money. Written in a relaxed, park-bench chat style, *The Money Chimp* makes the complex simple, and shows that you don't have to be a reader of the *Financial Times* to learn to implement the habits and skills of good money management. Reading it will be one of the best decisions you ever make."

Charles Hammond
Pastor, *Elim Pentecostal Church, West London*

"So many young people turn to credit cards to temporarily achieve a sense of freedom. Learn Andrew's five skills and five habits and you will achieve a life free from debt and anxiety. This is a must-read for every young person and every adult struggling to get out from under their debt."

Shirley McKinnon
Author of *Coach Yourself to Wealth*

"*The Money Chimp* is an insightful and actionable guidebook that will not only inspire you but also instruct you on how to make and manage your money. This is essential reading for anyone looking for clearly defined strategies on how to financially move forward and create a clear game plan. As a mother of six and grandmother of five *Money Chimp* hits the mark."

Sharon Tan
Living with Purpose Coach and Speaker

"I have been an adviser 26 years and read more books on this subject than I care to recall. Most are dry and academic and over-complicated. *The Money Chimp* however manages to address money issues in a logical fashion with an easy to follow structure.

"This little book addresses the core of money management and offers readers realistic and practical solutions. I have no doubt it will have a huge impact on people's lives."

Susan Bryant, Principal/Financial Adviser
Seeds of Advice, Financial Planning for Rural Families

"If you require an easy to understand book that highlights all the key areas to help you make and retain money, then buy this book."

Nicholas Charles FCCA
The Charles Group UK

What people say about *The Money Chimp* test

"I am a financial planner and *The Money Chimp* test is bang on target. Brilliant." **Ken**, Financial Advisor

"It was frighteningly accurate and gave me the big wake-up call I needed to sort out my finances."

Steven, Software designer

"The report described my money managing skills to a tee and highlighted the blind spots with practical recommendations." **Errol**, Life Skills trainer

"Amazing! Totally grabbed the attention of my 19 and 25 year olds."

Mark, Father of two young adults

The Money Chimp

Andrew Priestley

WRITING MATTERS PUBLISHING

The Money Chimp

First published in 2016

Writing Matters Publishing
10 Lovelace Court
Bethersden Kent UK TN26 3AY

info@writingmatterspublishing.com
www.writingmatterspublishing.com

Layout by Writing Matters Publishing
Edited by Diane Priestley
Cartoons by Andrew Priestley

ISBN 978-0-9575440-7-9 (pbk)

Please Note: *The Money Chimp* and *The Money Chimp* online test are intended as information only and do not constitute specific financial, investment, taxation or legal advice unique to your situation. It is for educational purposes only. Its sole aim is to help you become better at understanding managing your own money. The Author, Publisher and Resellers accept no responsibility for loss, damage or injury to persons or their belongings as a direct or indirect result of reading this book.

Dedication

This book is dedicated to all young people
who want to master money and build
a solid financial foundation for life!

And to all those with the courage
to choose financial freedom.

Contents

The Money Chimp at a glance and why you should read it

Extensive review
The Money Chimp is the result of an extensive review of money management books, websites and courses.

10 Money Managing Habits and Skills
The review identified five key money managing habits *(earning, spending, saving, investing, giving)* and five practical skills *(monitoring, focusing, reducing, training and taking action)*. Most people focus on *earning* and *spending* but neglect the other eight skills.

18-25s (and older) can be debt-free in 90 days
The book is geared towards 18-25s because typically they spend 130% of their weekly income and are the most likely to enter a cycle of debt. But it is suited for anyone who needs to manage their money more effectively and even become debt-free within 90 days.

You might be single or in a relationship. If you are single the challenge is take charge of your finances while you are independent and answerable only to yourself. If you are in a relationship, it's important to openly discuss financial issues with your partner and master these skills together.

Road-tested live in workshops

All material, activities and practical suggestions were road-tested in one-day workshops and three-month courses. No matter how interesting, if an idea didn't work in a live workshop, *it's not in this book*.

Pounds and dollars

The author works in the UK, Australia and the USA and the examples are a mixture of pounds and dollars.

Take the online test

You can rate your strengths in the 10 money managing principles by taking *The Money Chimp test* at:

www.moneychimp.net

Get a comprehensive report

The Money Chimp test includes 35 questions that generate a comprehensive 20-page money-managing report with practical recommendations and options.

Personalised feedback

The report is helpful because you get personalised feedback to every question you answer.

Award winning, #1 ranked author

Andrew Priestley is an award-winning, qualified business coach with over 17 years experience. His goal is to help business owners understand both business and personal finance.

He is the author of two other books on achieving financial and business success: *How Money Flows Through Your Business* and the #1 ranked business book *Starting*.

Part 1

Before we get started

Monkey magic

I remember Christmas, 1965 because I got a fantastic game called *Barrel of Monkeys* from Santa that is as popular now as it was then.

You get a little barrel containing 12 plastic monkeys with big curly arms. You start the game by shaking up the barrel and tipping out the monkeys. Then you pick up a monkey and use that monkey's arms to pick up another monkey. Then you use that second monkey to link to a third and so on.

You get a point for every monkey picked up but if you drop a monkey it's the next player's turn. The winner is the player with the most points. The winner is a *champ* and the losers are *chumps*!

It's exciting fun but it's a game of skill and harder than it sounds. You have to proceed carefully. And to win you have to think about what you are doing.

My personal best was six monkeys but the world speed record holder linked all 12 monkeys in about two minutes. (For your reference the record breaker was a 50 year old doctor!)

Managing your money is a lot like *Barrel of Monkeys:* a game of skill that takes practice.

The rules aren't difficult but likewise you have to keep playing and think about what you are doing. You might need to proceed slowly and be willing to learn from mistakes. And like any board game, such as *Monopoly, Cashflow 101,* or digital console games, the more you play the better you get.

And based on your results you are either a *champ* or a *chump.*

Winning is a challenge but as your skills develop you start winning and having more fun. Losing is very predictable if you rush and don't think about what you're doing.

Managing your money is just as fun as any kids game but the stakes are a lot higher.

Like a game, you can learn from experience and your mistakes but the fastest way to start winning is to learn the rules. The good news is managing your money has some basic rules that are easy to learn.

Once you start playing by the rules you start winning the money managing game, and life gets better. Want to know the rules? Then keep reading!

Are you a champ
or a chump with money?

Get a pen and underline any of the questions below that sound like you.

- *Are you careless with spending?*
- *Are you poor at managing money?*
- *Do you earn enough?*
- *Do you have problems budgeting?*
- *Are you hopeless at saving?*
- *Do you feel there's never enough?*
- *Do you watch TV shows of the rich and famous then feel envious or cynical about people who earn big bucks?*
- *Do you feel annoyed when ordinary people win millions on the lottery?*
- *Do you think it's unfair that you didn't?*

- *Do you feel unlucky?*
- *Do you wonder where all your money goes?*
- *Does money slip through your fingers like sand?*
- *Do you run out of money before the next payday?*
- *Does it usually feel like there is more month than money?*
- *Do you waste money on stuff you don't really need?*
- *Do you borrow money from family or friends?*
- *Do you spend too much on credit at Christmas?*
- *Do you often 'max out' your credit card?*
- *Are you usually late paying bills?*
- *Do you usually incur late fees?*

If you answered YES to just one of these questions – and I really do mean *just one* – then this book is for you.

You will discover 10 time-tested principles for managing money that can even have you debt-free within 90 days if you apply what you learn.

This is really useful information for *anyone* who needs to manage their money better but *The Money Chimp* is especially relevant for 18-25 year olds because they are the most likely to waste money and enter a cycle of chronic debt.

But why are young adults so prone to debt?

The end of the tunnel

We are just starting to come out of a global financial crisis (GFC) that started in 2009. But young people in *any* economy are under immense pressure to part with their cash - *and even go into debt* - to own the latest and greatest.

According to the charity *Mybnk*, 90% of Brits have no financial education; and youth debt is a staggering £8.3bn a year problem. That's why *Mybnk* specialises in educating young people about how to manage their money and even how to set up their own enterprise.

UK wealth coach, Simon Jeffries says, "The younger generation do not like to think about money until they are in their late 20s. They want to party! They live by the acronym *FOMO - Fear Of Missing Out* - even if that puts them into debt."

The problem is 18-25s are now the most likely to enter a chronic cycle of crippling debt unless they change their habits, skills and attitudes around money.

I was motivated to write this book because I know bright, aspiring young people in this age group. And I do not want them to ever stress and struggle over money, now or later in life.

Over several years I read books and online articles and attended courses on managing money and identified 10 recurring principles. You might already know some of the ideas in this book but I am sure some ideas will be brand new to you.

But I believe that this is the first time these 10 proven money-managing principles have all appeared in the one book and in this unique format.

You will discover 10 time-tested principles designed to get you debt-free in the next 90 days.

If you are in the 18-25 age zone then this book might just save you time, money and stress. And it might make you debt-free, financially free and wealthier.

But the principles in this book aren't just for young adults. They apply to *anyone* of *any age* with poor attitudes, habits and skills around money.

In addition to the book, you can take *The Money Chimp* test online to see *exactly* how you rate *right now* in these 10 principles.

The Money Chimp test takes about seven minutes to complete online and you immediately get back a comprehensive, personalised PDF money managing report. You can take the test right now at:

www.moneychimp.net

The truth about most
18-25 year olds and money

Do you know most 18-25 year olds spend 130% of their weekly *disposable income*. If you earn a £100 a week this means you spend £130, on average. But how is that possible?

Well, you will spend money on food shopping, rent, utilities and transport, right? But then there's your *discretionary income* - money available to save, invest or spend after you've paid your bills, necessities and taxes. What do you spend that money on?

Typically most of your discretionary money is spent on things you can't afford and don't really need powered by an ingrained *have now and pay later* mentality.

Typically you are about two paydays - four if you are lucky - from being flat broke. If you usually live beyond your means you'll have this fantasy of getting a better job, a pay rise, winning the lottery or receiving a windfall (inheritance).

The truth is most young people get into the habit of being bailed out by some benevolent person (usually their mum or dad, relatives or friends). Or if you are like most young adults you get into the habit of misusing a credit card.

Sadly, most young people have never been taught how to do the most important life skill ever – managing your money. And so pretty soon, you are spending more than you earn and most likely racking up credit card debt plus the interest, fees and charges that go with misusing bank credit.

This describes most older people too. A recent survey said 89% of wage earners *of any age group* can't maintain their lifestyle beyond six weeks if they lose their job. If this sounds like you, then unless you change, you might experience the effect of poor money habits, too.

The good news is you can change! The principles in this book are timeless, applicable to you, easy to learn and really useful.

But before we go any further I want to give you an interesting little exercise that involves some web searching.

A picture is worth a thousand words

I am interested in the personal finances of people living in three Western economies – the UK, USA and Australia. So, let's start with those three countries. I want you to fire up your web browser and type in UK, USA or Australian *spending habits infographic.*

I've selected these three countries because their governments publish reasonably accurate and up-to-date economic data related to average household income and expenditure.

An infographic displays complex information as a picture rather than reams of text and data. I like infographics because you can quickly see what's happening at a glance rather than having to wade through a written report.

I found an infographic produced by the *Australian Securities and Investment Commission* (ASIC) very interesting. You can quickly see what most 'ordinary' householders are doing with their income.

In that year, the total annual household income was AUD$642 billion. And how they spent that money is fascinating. For example, Australians spent $2.7 billion on vegetables and $5.4 billion on chocolate, and $9.5 billion on dental!

They spent $10 billion on beauty, $9 billion on gadgets, $5 billion on fashion, $2.68 billion going to the cinema but only $2 billion on education and $0.78 billion on self-improvement.

We can infer Australians need to make some better spending choices.

The UK infographic is equally fascinating. It shows Brits earn on average £27.6K per annum and their highest expenses are housing, transport and food.

I was interested in how Brits spend their discretionary income (money left over after paying household bills). Apparently, music is a high priority in Northern Ireland, sport is the highest discretionary expenditure in the north of England and Londoners spend the most on beauty treatments!

There is a revealing infographic that shows that 18-25s are the most susceptible to debt, 35-45s have the least amount of discretionary spend and 54-65s are the best savers.

The USA householder stats show similar patterns.

So, the activity is to get *Googling*. Make sure you click on the *Images* tab and include the word *infographic* in your search.

Start with Australia, UK and USA because I know you will find some useful infographics. By the way, I looked at infographics over the past five years and it seems spending patterns have not changed much.

If you don't live in these three countries, Google *your* country and see what you can find. I'll wait.

OK, you're back. So what did you discover and what does all this mean to you?

Well firstly, it should give you an indication of how much people in your country currently earn and what they spend their money on annually. And therefore because you live in that country what you might also expect to earn and spend.

Obviously, there are exceptions to the national averages but for now all we need is a thought provoking snapshot and a heads-up.

The average UK income is currently £27,600. Tax aside, if you spent 130% of that income you would have spent £35,880 - an additional £8,280! A lot of that is in the form of debt.

And of concern, studies say this is the norm.

The Money Chimp gets you to explore two important questions. Firstly, what do you spend your money on?

You need to know.

And: is there a possibility that you can actually spend less than you earn so that you are not just breaking even but creating surplus cash?

And the answer is 'yes'. It is very possible.

I want to emphasise that there is so much useful information on the web about managing your money, personal finance, budgeting, saving money, reducing debt and so on. And I was surprised by the amount of first-rate, free, online personal finance courses, too. All you need to do is search.

But start by looking at infographics.

I think I am skilled at managing my personal finances but even I got some useful tips on how to improve things by looking at the householder data from several countries.

Starting with eating less chocolate!

The three top
money-managing tips

Money works along fixed principles of cause and effect and the principles are straightforward and easy to understand. The right way to manage your money is time-tested, proven and established. We know what works and what doesn't.

I did a search on the top money managing tips of all time. They are:

1. Spend less that you earn
2. Plan for the future and
3. Make your money make *more* money.

Let's look at each principle in more detail.

Money Tip #1
Spend less than you earn

The most sensible money management tip has to be:

Don't spend more than you earn

In Charles Dickens' classic novel *David Copperfield,* the character Wilkins Micawber gives the much quoted recipe for happiness:

> "Annual income twenty pounds, annual expenditure nineteen, nineteen and six, result happiness.
> Annual income twenty pounds, annual expenditure twenty pounds ought and six, result misery."

In plain English, no matter what century you live in, if you earn £20 and spend less than £20 you are OK. If you earn £20 and spend more, you are in trouble!

In these days of easy credit, I would probably amend this advice to:

**Don't spend more money
than you can afford to repay**

When *David Copperfield* was written in 1850 the general public did not have access to banking, lending and personal finance tools such as credit cards and personal loans that we have today.

There is a difference between *good* and *bad* debt. Taking a mortgage on a family home is *good debt* (or any borrowings that are tax deductible), whereas borrowing money to buy expensive wearable technology or a new car qualifies as *bad debt*.

A mortgage is considered *good debt* because a house is an investment that can go up in value and yield profit when sold in the future (but not always); while borrowing to purchase consumer items is considered *bad debt* because these items usually decrease in resale value.

There is a lot to be said for living within your current means. This does not mean you should accept your current level of income. Aim to improve your current income but at any level aim to live below that level. In fact, aim to create a *surplus of cash*.

Money Tip #2
Plan for the future

It makes sense to plan for future financial needs. But I understand that when you are 18 it is hard enough imagining being 25 or 30 let alone trying to imagine a time when you will be old and grey in your 60s or 70s retired and living on a pension (if pensions will even exist in your future) Subsequently, most young people can't be bothered planning.

Most young people say, "I'll make the money first *and then* I'll plan for the future." But every money expert says the time to plan for the future is as early as possible.

I recently heard of a bright, young, hard working computer coder who started his own business. His income has grown from £24k to £84k a year and he has bought a small apartment. Wisely he has invested in ISAs and a pension scheme and is on target to being financially independent by his early 40s.

He may be an exception to the rule but the point is: *think about your future, now.*

Back to the future again

The future is a lot more predictable than we think (flying cars, self lacing trainers and hover boards aside.)

Most governments have something like a *national bureau of statistics* that identifies short and long-range trends. They carefully analyse these trends to plan ahead.

There is a phenomenon called the *Baby Boomers,* the generation born between the years 1946 and 1964. After the Second World War (1945) there was a massive spike in the population unlike anything seen before.

Imagine a python swallowed a pig whole. You would see this huge bump as that pig slowly passes through the digestive tract inside the body of the python.

Well, that's how economist David Cork imagined the *Baby Boomer* phenomenon. The pig is the *Baby Boomers* and the python is a time line. Cork's book, *The Pig and The Python,* explores the economic trends associated with *Baby Boomers* as they age and move through time.

He suggests that the most profitable trends have always been associated with the current age of the boomers. So when the *Boomers* were infants baby wear boomed. When the *Boomers* went to school education boomed. When the *Boomers* became teenagers, teen fashion and music boomed. As adults, the *Boomers* needed housing and food so housing and supermarkets boomed. Therefore any stocks and shares associated *with those trends* also boomed.

The first of the *Boomers* turned 70 in 2016 and the big money making trends should include things such as aged care, medtech, biotech, nutrition, tourism, private gated communities and retirement finance.

Governments are also looking closely at these trends because they need to fund infrastructure and support.

As more people are exiting the workforce, there will be less taxpayers and that will place a massive financial drain on governments. That's why they are extending the retirement age, reducing welfare, eliminating pensions and aged benefits and introducing new laws and tax incentives for workplace and self-funded pension schemes.

The question at any age is: *Do I have enough money?* More so if you are thinking ahead to retiring.

In Lee Eisenberg's book *The Number* he asks, "What do you need financially for the rest of your life and what will it cost to retire?" This book is not for the faint-hearted. If you think that one day you will retire with a pension and have enough to live on, think again. Most likely you will need to self-fund your retirement and lifestyle because most Western governments are going to phase out pensions and state benefits.

Even the key message of a much softer guide to planning for the future *Planning for Retirement* by Patrick Grant can be summed up by saying the sooner you start saving money in a pension scheme the more money you will have when you retire. Start now!

National Bureaus of Statistics can suggest how your life will run from cradle to the grave because they have the research data and have analysed the trends in order to plan for the future needs of the population.

A great example of forward planning is the vast amount of money London is spending on developing the new inner city cross rail links and nationwide high speed train networks, now, in anticipation of growing needs 25 years from now.

Even the London Underground is upgrading a 50 year old signalling system to meet demands 50 years from now.

However, governments now want you to do your bit in planning your financial future. In fact, you may not have a choice.

Cradle to grave

So here are the stages of life flagged by national bureaus of statistics that will cost big money and require you to plan ahead.

Childhood and teens - education
In Western countries you will go into child care, then kindergarten and then primary school. Then you will go to secondary school. You will need bassinets and prams and bikes and uniforms and dental and sports equipment and toys … and stuff … and more stuff kids need and want.

At about 17 you will either go on to do tertiary education, adult education, get an apprenticeship, seek employment or you will start your own business. I assume you do not have ambitions to become a career welfare benefits recipient.

Adolescence to early adult
If you go down the tertiary education/apprenticeship route you will finish education or training by about 23.

Some will complete education later, if you take a gap year or defer for a time. Many young adults are keen to travel in early to mid 20s and often take a gap year to explore the world.

From 18, trying out adulthood, exploring relationships and getting established in work takes priority.

Statistically, by late 20s you might still looking for the right job and emotionally and biologically you are looking for the right partner. Some partner younger of course, but it appears this generation is finding Mr or Miss Right later.

And they are marrying (or civil partnering) later. Marriage used to be popular in the early 20s, then mid to late 20s and now weddings are often postponed until early 30s.

Statistics show that 18-25s are the most susceptible to chronic debt. If you go to university you will most likely graduate with a student loan debt that on average takes another seven years to pay off.

By late 20s you have probably stabilised your job and partner search and you are most probably looking for a home of your own especially if you've found your mate.

Millenials (Gen X and Gen Ys born from 1982 to early 2004) is the next major population trend (also called *Echo Boomers*). This new generation is more interested in experiences and rental accommodation than home ownership.

They spend up big on fashion, gadgets and technology, socialising and travel. And that is why experts see this generation as highly susceptible to credit card debt.

Adulthood and new family (35-45s)

At this stage you are now thinking about a home loan. If you are 35 plus and take a 25-year mortgage you are expecting to carry that burden until around age 60.

However, rarely will you stay in the same house. You may even sell that home at a profit and use the equity gained to finance your next home. We used to move homes every 10 years but now it's about every seven years. On this basis you will probably mortgage at least three to four family homes in your lifetime.

At this stage couples are thinking about starting a family and medically there is now pressure to have children before you reach your 40s.

A priority will be stabilising your income because you need to pay for child care, kindergarten, primary and secondary school, medical, dental etc. Insurances start to make a lot more sense. (If you have a mortgage, house insurance will probably be a condition of the loan.)

People in the 35-45 age range have the least amount of disposable income and as stated 18-25s are the most likely to be in a cycle of bad debt entering that age zone.

Even though retirement seems way off it is probably a good idea to start thinking about your pension pot.

Locate 'lost' pensions

You have probably already worked in several jobs and acquired several pension schemes without even knowing you were enrolled in one. It's money you don't even know you have. Helping people find and consolidate their *lost* pension funds is now a growth industry.

You can help yourself by first compiling a list of all your past jobs. Maybe you have a tidy small sum already!

Most taxation departments offer a free online service to locate and consolidate lost pension schemes. You don't need to pay for this service and it's well worth the effort.

I know of a couple in their late 40s who found over £47,000 *each,* spread across several schemes! What a windfall! That's money they didn't realise they had.

Pre-retirement (55+)

If you started your family at 35, your children will be hitting their 20s by the time you're 55. You have probably paid off your mortgage.

This age group has the most *disposable income* and if you missed out on travel in your 20s you are probably going to see the world in your 50s and 60s and you can afford to travel in comfort.

If you were sensible you also started planning for retirement in your early 40s at the latest. However, many people put off planning until late 40s. As a result most people will be forced to work until their early 70s because they cannot afford to retire.

Retirement and old age (70 plus)

Hopefully, you've earned and saved enough to support yourself and your lifestyle in your retirement and old age when health and aged care are sure to become a priority.

An emerging trend will be *Baby Boomer*s downsizing to much smaller homes or moving into aged care. Boomers might need to fund their retirement this way.

Experts predict this will impact housing prices.

We're living longer but we are not staying as healthy due to obesity, diabetes, cancer, heart disease and other illnesses so it appears you might need to also factor in the cost of prolonged health care.

And that's how the experts predict your life unfolding financially. Knowing this is highly predictable should encourage you to consider your needs going forward. I hope as you read on you will discover you have the power to take charge of every stage of your life.

Time to put the book down for a minute

I suggest you reread the last section because there's a lot to absorb. This will make sense to older readers who might be feeling nervous about their financial security. I don't expect younger readers to emotionally connect with these concerns just yet but you should still be aware that these are predictable trends that most likely will affect your life sooner or later.

And if any of you *Millennials* are this far into the book it suggests you are quite mature for your age.

Take a few moments to consider what this means to you. And when you're ready join me in the next chapter for some good news.

These predictions
are not fixed in concrete

None of these predictions are fixed in concrete even though these stages are statistically common.

Obviously you will be focusing on the stage you are in right now. Asking you to plan for your retirement at 22 seems a long way off and probably doesn't make any sense whatsoever, does it?

But the common thread through *any* life stage however is: *do I have enough money?* Smart people start thinking about money management sooner and they plan ahead.

Even doing something as simple as forming the habit of saving 10% of your after-tax, income will have a positive benefit in the future.

I first learned the concept of saving 10% of your after-tax, income from the George Clason who wrote the *The Richest Man in Babylon,* which is now a classic.

My wife and I still save 10% of our after-tax income and therefore we always have savings. But for many people saving is not yet a habit or a goal.

I'm going to suggest that you try it. Save 10% of your take home pay for the next three months so that you start to get a sense that saving money and planning ahead is possible and beneficial.

Those people who *financially* navigate each of the stages of life well have consciously developed habits and skills in earning, spending (budgeting), saving (creating surplus), investing (leveraged spending) and giving.

And they have learned to monitor their income and expenditure, control spending, focus and budget where needed, set goals and targets and importantly take action.

Even small plans and actions can yield satisfying results. The key difference between those with enough money and those without enough money – lucky windfalls aside – is knowing how much is *enough*. And then taking appropriate action even if that involves discipline and sacrifices.

Learning how to manage your money is probably the skill that will have the most positive impact on your entire life.

I read recently of a couple who had racked up credit card debts of over £41,000. To them credit card debt was considered *normal*.

Using principles like those in this book, they reduced that debt to zero. But make no mistake, it took 22 months of smart thinking, discipline, hard work and going without.

I recently chatted with a young couple who over many months managed to become debt-free.

"For a long time we ignored the problem. Eventually, we accepted we were in trouble and could no longer ignore the obvious. But the stress of the debt had to get *really* bad before we were finally motivated to even look at a website on money management.

"What shocked us was how useful even the simplest ideas were and how much useful information had been *freely available* to us *at any time*. But we were the victim of our poor attitudes to money, bad habits and lack of skills."

The point is your future is highly predictable and your bad money habits can come with a high price tag. But learning good money habits and skills can change your entire life for the better.

You need to know what works. And you have to be ready and willing to change.

Money Tip #3
Make your money make *more* money

Quick review. The top money tips so far are:

1. Don't spend more than you earn or can afford to repay and
2. Plan for the future.

It is true that money makes more money but only under certain conditions. For example, reckless gambling or buying a lottery ticket may not yield any result whatsoever and may even leave you worse off. The four *'money makes more money'* methods that work reliably are *cash, shares, property* and *businesses*.

Several years ago I had $10,000 in an Australian bank savings account, that, after 12 months earned me $3.06 in interest. That pathetic return didn't even buy a glass of beer! But if I had millions to park in a bank I'd carefully pick something with a much better rate of return than .001%. Banks used to be the place to save money but right now savers are worse off leaving hard earned money in a low interest bearing personal account.

By contrast, in 1982, my wife Diane and I saved up $7,000 in Australia for a deposit on a house and paid $18,000 for our first home. Four years later in 1986 we sold it for $65,000. After we repaid our mortgage we had $54,000 equity and bought a $99,000 home which we later sold in 1989 for $151,000.

Maybe we're the generation that feels safer with bricks and mortar but property has always been a good investment for us.

Globally there has been what's termed a *bull run* on property for over 20 years which experts say cannot continue so this means the returns you expect from property might not be as high in the future.

I know of a young man that loves shares. He bought his first share portfolio in his early 20s and his portfolio has grown steadily over time.

I love businesses. Where else can you take seed capital of $500 and turn that into $32,000? It took a year, but that accurately describes my first business.

Apparently *Millennials* are quite entrepreneurial and like businesses, too. I ran a money-managing workshop with a group of young people and most of their questions were about starting a business.

While they might have a good idea for a business, few have a good business for the idea. We know this because 80% of business start-ups fail within the first two years and poor financial knowledge is often a factor in the failure.

I wrote a book called *Starting!* that shows you how to you make sure you have a viable business idea before you start trading. (It's on *Amazon*.)

But you don't need to start a full-blown business. It can be part time hobby business.

At one time I was buying and selling old books on *eBay*. I found an old first edition Enid Blyton *Noddy* book for £4 and sold it for £80. Some people make good money buying and selling on *eBay* but you need to know exactly what you are doing.

One of the attendees at a workshop liked the idea of buying low and selling higher. He started selling *X-Box* and *Playstation* games on *eBay*. He would buy them for a few pounds and on-sell them for £15 to 20.

Clearly, there's more to *'making money make more money'* – a book in itself. My little $500 investment in a business wasn't a gamble. I knew exactly what I needed to do to leverage $500. It was not wishful thinking. And the little house we bought certainly paid dividends.

But that's the key point. You need to educate yourself. You have to know what you are doing. You need to learn new habits and skills that work. And I know you don't need this book to tell you the obvious. Most people I meet know they need to sort out their finances. And they fully intend to get cracking.

But they don't because they run into two obstacles.

Two big show stoppers

Two key roadblocks to taking action and effectively managing your money are *legitimate obstacles* and *self-imposed limitations.*

#1 Legitimate obstacles
There are several legitimate reasons why some people cannot manage their finances.

Some people have diminished physical or mental capacity. Joel is 29 and profoundly disabled and can't even move unassisted let alone read a credit card statement.

Other people are coping with difficult circumstances such as downturns in the economy and being made redundant through industry closures (such as mining or steel works).

Others live in poor countries or face living with war or natural disasters.

My great-grandfather was a house painter and when the local coal mines shut down there was no work for anyone. He moved from Yorkshire to London to find work but those who stayed behind fell into abject poverty and misery.

If anything like that sounds like your experience then you probably *will* struggle to manage your finances. However, there are countless stories of people who overcame incredible odds and succeeded.

#2 Self-Imposed Limitations

Most experts say that your ability to manage money can be diminished by self-imposed limitations. For whatever reason you have convinced yourself that you're *no good with money*.

You can of course change the way you think about money at any time and wealth coaches help people change their circumstances by changing their core beliefs and behaviours.

Family influences

There is a TV show in the UK about families who are second and third generation welfare recipients called *Life on Benefits*.

The people featured in the programme are usually angry at someone. They blame the government, they blame rich people, they blame other welfare recipients but mostly they blame their family. And while they have a long list of who to blame, often they are not on their own list.

Often they say things like, "The reason I'm broke is because my mum and dad were always broke."

Not everyone blames their parents or their upbringing or sees a hopeless future of being 'broke like mum and dad.' You might have to work hard but you still have options.

I recently met a successful young entrepreneur who said, "The reason I'm wealthy is *because my mum and dad were always broke.*"

The point is everyone has values, beliefs, attitudes and habits about money learned growing up.

I grew up in a family that did not have much money. If I wanted to buy something I had to first decide if I really *needed it* or just *wanted it.*

My parents asked, "Andrew, do you *need it* or *want it*?"

I had to explain why I needed it. If I proved that I needed it then I worked for pocket money, saved up or paid it off in instalments. That's how I bought my first bike. This is an example of delayed gratification, a lesson I learned quite young. And how I appreciated and enjoyed my bicycle!

Our family didn't take bank loans, borrow money or use credit cards.

My grandparents lived through World War 1, and along with their children – my parents - they lived through the Great Depression of the early 1930s and then World War 2 in the 1940s. My parents then came through Post-War 1950s UK with food stamps and rations. They had a better time in the 1960s but then struggled through the recession of the 1970s.

So I am sure a lot of their worries about money rubbed off on me when I was growing up.

Even though the Second World War was at least 15 years over when I was a child we had to eat everything on our plate (including the pattern) and there was no dessert until we did. We were taught not to waste anything. And there were no snacks or fast food treats in between meals.

Sometimes I still eat like I'm on post-war rations! These days, in many cultures, it's polite and healthy to *leave* some food on your plate. So it's important to review and adjust those childhood beliefs and automatic behaviours.

I am sure you have influences like mine that underpin your relationship with money that need reviewing.

The economy had changed by the time I became a parent. Our kids have no concerns spending money. They buy whatever they want, when they want it. And they throw stuff away easily. And even though *I now have enough money* I am still very careful about what I buy and throw away.

My friend Ken the financial advisor says there are two types of investors: those who invest because of fear (fear of losing what they've got) and those who invest because of optimism and opportunities (excitement about gaining more.) I'm probably the former.

But I admire a famous entrepreneur who said he had two goals in life: one to make his fortune and the other to double it.

I grew up believing if you wanted something you worked for it. But the people in the TV show on welfare *resent* that they have to work for money. They believe the government owes them a living. And if you grow up in that environment it is very hard to change that mind-set.

Your money mind-set or *software*

Not surprisingly you develop your mind-set about money at an early age. In a sense, when you were a kid you wrote some mental *life software* on how money works. In most cases, you haven't upgraded your software for years or ever! Maybe you are still running very old software.

You wouldn't run *Windows 4* or *OS 3* if your computer requires *Windows 10* or *OS 11*, right?

If you've got money worries it might suggest your internal 'money software' is due for an upgrade!

Or maybe you've downloaded someone else's money software - like your parents - and you're just running theirs while believing it's yours!

My parents were most emphatic, "Don't waste money." And they thought borrowing money from a bank was risky. But they grew up through the Depression and a World War. Is it any wonder that *I hate wasting money* and err on the side of financial caution. Job done!

That's why most wealth coaches will ask you to write a *money biography* that explores the messages, rules and even admonitions you received as a child. And trust me, you do have a money mind-set. We all do.

The voice recorder activity

This is a great activity you can do yourself using the voice recorder app on your smart phone.

Turn on the recorder and answer this one question: *what is money?*

Keep asking *the same* question over and over and make sure you record whatever answers comes up.

What is money?

I did this activity for over an hour and was surprised at what beliefs are sitting just below the surface.

This simple activity will give you an indication of your *money software.*

That software will include fears and attitudes that translate into very powerful beliefs such as 'There's not enough to go round'; 'Be careful with money'; 'You are bad if you waste money'; 'Easy come easy go'; 'You can have anything you want'; 'If you love me you will spend money on me' and so on.

There are thousands of beliefs we form about money as children that continue to influence us as adults. By flushing out these old beliefs you will identify beliefs that work and those you need to change.

Many people believe they are *no good at managing money and never will be.* But this is totally false. In fact it's a lie. You can learn new financial attitudes and skills and be responsible with money at *any time* and *any age.* Right?

OK, I'm stuck

Now if you believe there is *absolutely nothing* you can do to change your situation, then understand, you are highly committed to *that option.*

And once that happens you have an excuse! There is no point to even bother trying to manage your money wisely.

We all act on what we believe to be true. If you believe you are hopeless with money then you just learn to accept that there will always be *more month than money.* And you will procrastinate and abdicate responsibility, and promise yourself to sort it one day and that things will be better as soon as you get a pay rise, or a new job, or win the lottery or get an inheritance.

You might imagine that next Friday night you expect to win the $133 million lottery jackpot. And the tooth fairy and a luck genie is your back-up plan. Right?

By the way, most people who win the lottery are broke within 18 months, because while their financial circumstances change, their attitudes and thinking -

and money software - don't. Most winners spend their millions or give it away to family and friends. Very few invest. Most end up in more debt.

Wealth coach, Karen Sutton-Johal understands debt better than anyone. She says that her childhood was essentially one financial disaster after another. That inspired her to become a debt adviser. But she noticed that people who get out of debt will go straight back into debt primarily because they don't change their mind-set.

A wealth coach will challenge your current beliefs and mind-set and in most cases once your mind-set changes you will manage your money better.

If you say things like, "I can't get my head around money" or "I can't learn this" or "I'm no good at budgeting …" a wealth coach will ask, "Because … ?" to check if your reasons are legitimate, self-imposed or just 'old software'.

Money saving expert, Martin Lewis says that improving your finances might be as simple as challenging the most basic of long-held beliefs such as 'Stay loyal to your existing suppliers' (no, shop around!) and 'Debt is bad' (no, *bad debt* is bad!).

As one wealth coach put it, "Money isn't just about having a head for figures. It's about understanding your beliefs and behaviours and the unconscious inheritance you've received from people and events in the past."

Let's talk about credit cards

I am big fan of credit cards when they are used as originally intended - as a short-term line of credit and interest-free if paid off by the due date. I normally use my credit card wisely and I usually pay off the balance when it falls due and so in most cases pay zero interest charges.

But most people struggle with crippling credit card debt. They don't pay off the amount due and needlessly incur interest, late fees and charges.

I recently read about a 29-year old executive who racked up £50,000 on credit cards. Can you even imagine getting a bank statement that says you owe £50,000 on your credit card? And given the *Annual Percentage Rate* (APR) was 27% can you see how fast she was going into long term debt?

It was manageable until one day she was made redundant and then like a house of cards her world fell apart. She divorced, lost her home and her car was repossessed. Finally she declared bankruptcy.

As an exercise she analysed 24 months of statements to see *exactly* what she'd spent £50,000 on. The results were shocking.

It came down to buying gadgets and the latest designer label clothing and accessories - stuff that never lasted. And the key driver was to impress others.

Access to credit

Did you know that in the early 1970s women could not get a loan or a credit card without their father or husband giving permission or acting as guarantor?

That all changed with the introduction of laws like the *Equal Pay* and *Sex Discrimination Acts of 1975* (UK).

Are men are better at managing money? No, the ability to manage money is not gender specific. It's a skill both genders can and should master. Men get into chronic debt just as quickly and easily as women.

Impulse control

But access to credit has overridden two important psychological drivers; impulse control and the ability to delay gratification. This is what we are trying to teach children when we toilet train them, teach them to do homework before television, or eat their vegetables before they have dessert. Impulse says "I want it now!" and "I do not want to wait."

We know about this because Stanford University conducted a landmark study in the 1960s.

They sat four year olds in a room with a lolly and a bell on the table and said, "If you can just wait 15 minutes you can have *two* lollies. But if you want one lolly, right now, ring the bell."

And that's a tough challenge for any four year old.

Here's what happened. A lot of kids rang the bell straight away and ate the lolly. Other kids resisted for a short time and then ate the lolly. But a lot of kids found ways to *not* eat the lolly. They distracted themselves. They sang songs or looked away. And after what must have seemed an eternity, *they got two lollies!*

Those children were then observed over 20 years. The kids that *waited* were consistently more successful in *all* endeavours of life than the kids that couldn't wait.

And this is culturally robust meaning wherever this experiment is conducted in the world they get a similar result.

But a credit card is like saying, 'Here's the lolly. Don't wait. Eat it now. Pay later.'

Credit cards give you the power to let you have what you want - *now! And that feels good.* Most of us engage in *retail therapy* from time to time.

And the science confirms it is hard to say 'No' when it's incredibly easy to say 'Yes'. The problem is credit cards let you spend a lot more than you ever intended.

So a wealth coach will help you look at what you use your credit card for, how you can use it more wisely and hopefully how to stay debt-free in the process.

But the message is clear: you must learn to delay gratification and control your impulse to spend.

I like credit cards and use them to pay for a range of things like fuel, train tickets, meals and so on. But I pay the balance when it falls due so I take full advantage of 55 days interest-free credit. And I have good cash flow. It only works because I pay off the credit card when it falls due each month.

But what if you can't pay it all off?

A simple idea when reducing credit card debt is to focus on the smallest debts first and get rid of those. For example, I took three months to gradually pay off an airline ticket but paid all the minor charges off on time.

Some wealth experts say the best way to reduce credit card debt is to stop using your credit card. They even suggest putting your credit card in the freezer!

If you can't manage your impulse to spend, cut up your credit cards so you stop incurring more debt.

Listen to your money talk

When I listen to people talk about money they either *sound and act like a kid* or they *sound and act like a grown up*.

If people say things like, "*I can't … I haven't … I must … I should … it's too late … money is so boring … I hate saving … I just wanna … I'm helpless … I'm no good … I don't want to … yes but … I'm scared to look … why are we doing this anyway? … I've got to*" then typically I am dealing with someone who is emotionally young in the way they think about money.

And they usually act helpless and even scared around money. Regardless of their chronological age when the topic turns to saving or budgeting they go child-like. They glaze over and the shutters come down. Suddenly very smart people feel overwhelmed and find it hard to concentrate. If you are over 18 - legally an adult and responsible for your actions - and you sound like this, then you have a problem.

If someone says, *"I'm learning this ... I'm trying that ... I'm reading about ... I asked someone about ... I did a course ... I'm talking to my bank ... I set up ... I read my statements ... I'm learning how ... this is interesting ... I'll give that a go ... I plan to ..."* then typically I am talking to someone who is grown-up around money.

By the way I haven't said *adult* on purpose. It has little to do with your chronological age. The ability to manage your money is a *grown-up* skill. If it were an adult skill all adults would manage their money wisely. I know children who can manage their pocket money better than their parents.

The trick is to consider - *energetically* - whether you are more like a kid or a grown-up around money regardless of your chronological age.

Managing money is *grown ups'* work.

If you sense you are feeling like a kid - helpless or overwhelmed - then shut your eyes, take a few deep breaths and quietly repeat these magic words, "Leave this to me, this is grown-ups work." You will feel your energy and your thinking shift in a positive direction.

Part 2

The Five Habits and Five Skills

THE MONEY CHIMP

Is managing your money a science or an art?

Both. Money works along fixed principles that are so easy to understand and start using that anyone as young as an 18 year old can get it right. The money managing principles in this book are time-tested, proven and established.

We know exactly what works. For example:

Don't spend more than you earn

And while increasing your income and controlling your spending is important there are eight other principles.

If you follow these principles and apply them in most cases you will be financially better off within 90 days.

But here's the bad news.

While the principles are easy to understand they may require some smart thinking and hard work to start implementing. Why?

Because it might involve changing long-standing, ingrained habits, attitudes and beliefs and developing new skills. But changing anything requires conscious effort and often requires you to get uncomfortable.

Usually the way you are with money right now is nothing more than a habit. And habits are just that – activities you've done over and over again until they are automatic – even if those habits are well past their use-by date or based on information that was well out-of-date when you first learned it.

If you are in debt and doing nothing about it then you are saying, *"I'm no good at managing money and my only option is to be in debt." But* there's a problem with such a limiting option.

If you believe you are no good at managing money then you *now* have a good excuse for doing nothing. You will unconsciously decide not to look for other options like learning to manage your money or being cashed-up and debt-free. You'll argue, 'I'm no good at managing money.' So why even try?

But you *do* have other options and that involves making active choices.

Learning new skills takes commitment but right now you are committed. You are just committed to mismanaging your money and being in debt! You're committed to the wrong strategy!

This book gives you 10 proven money managing principles that you can use starting right away. Right now, today. And they work.

Here's some examples:

- Two sisters – both university students - were both debt-free in 90 days after applying just a little of what they learned.

- A drummer with a rock band was debt free within 90 days after applying what he learned here.

- An unemployed 19-year old on minimum wage of $4.27 per hour went on to create a little business that earns him $15 per hour, 8 hours a day, 5 days a week.

- A youth pastor went from being perpetually broke to bringing his finances under control within 90 days.

- A high-income earning doctor went from massive debt to finances under control within six months.

- A husband and wife of 30 years reduced their discretionary spending by £1,200 a month! Ironically, both worked as financial advisors!

- A couple with over £41,000 in credit card debts were debt free within 22 months.

- A single mum with $8,000 in credit card debt was debt free with 90 days.

While there is no guarantee, the 10 principles in this book should be helpful if you start to apply the simple suggestions.

While this book is not intended to resolve serious financial problems within 90 days like being £41,000 in debt, using these principles in conjunction with professional advice will certainly move you in the right direction.

These people were all making some of the top 10 mistakes. They all made a committed and sincere 90-day test of the ideas in this book. It did not require affirmations or the adoption of some nonsensical belief system. It required new skills and application.

They carefully explored the 10 principles and then took action.

Success was built on taking either small steps or drastic measures. But ultimately, they could see the steps they needed to take and they took them.

I propose to show you the top 10 money managing mistakes that you are making and explain what to do to fix those problems.

Your performance plan

If you want to improve *anything* in your life there are three things that consistently work:

- You have to STOP doing what doesn't work
- You have to START doing what does work; and
- You have to CONTINUE doing things that are working.

A university student, Melanie, had to STOP 'treating' herself. She had to STOP running up credit card debt to buy things like fashion, accessories, shoes, handbags and expensive beauty treatments.

She had to START to reduce her £9,000 credit card debt. Melanie STARTED to get serious about reducing debt by taking a second job to fast track that result. That second job was part-time, two nights a week on Fridays and Saturdays. Obviously her social life took a nose dive for a while.

And she had to CONTINUE that new habit. This became much easier once she saw that debt on credit card was reducing.

Once she got the credit card debt under control she had to CONTINUE doing what she was doing to keep it that way.

You might *relapse*. Relapse means going right back to the very habit that needed to be changed such as racking up credit card debt on fashion.

Relapse is actually highly predictable when you are trying to change a habit. If you want to read a brilliant book on changing just about anything read *Changing for Good*. Prochanska, Norcross and Diclemente's ground breaking research has been at the forefront of change for the last 40 years specifically as it applies to people with addictions. They say: *expect relapse*. Expecting *relapse* can help you avoid it.

I also asked Melanie to reflect on where she got the idea that 'treating herself' required expensive shopping expeditions. Turns out it's a social thing linked to being liked and approved of by her friends.

My client Troy runs a successful construction business but has an expensive recreational drug habit. When we talked it through it turns out that Tony gets approval from his mates because he is usually the one buying.

He says if he gives up drugs he won't get to party with his mates. And there is the addictive nature of the substance. But when Tony stepped in front of a fast moving taxi late one night none of his so-called *mates* came to see him for the six weeks he was in hospital recovering. Nor did they chip in for his medical bills.

At the heart of your problems with managing money are your beliefs about money. Here's proof. Try this exercise.

Most mobile phones have a voice recorder. For the next 20 minutes I want you to have the conversation about money that I mentioned earlier, again. Make sure you record your answers.

You can of course write them down but I've found recording your answers works better because I want you to listen back to this recording.

You keep asking yourself the same question and keep answering it with whatever comes to mind:

What is money?
Money is ...

Try it now. Answer the question. *What is money?* Money is struggle. *What is money?* Money is fun. *What is money?* Money is about paying bills. *What is money?* Money is going to pay for something and my card is declined. *What is money?* Money is responsibility. Get the idea? Just keep going.

Just say the first thing that comes to mind. I am sure you will find both positive and negative beliefs. The trick is not to give up too soon. Some people do this activity for about three minutes and then say, "OK, I get it. I have some stupid beliefs about money."

But don't stop. Keep going.

What is money?

The benefit comes in persisting. I have done this activity with many people and they feel totally depressed at first but as they continue with the exercise they gain powerful insights. They hear their fears and beliefs out loud.

By the way, this is a great activity to do with a trusted friend. Your friend however should not engage you in a discussion. They should let you talk but then ask, "What is money?" Just that question.

This activity uncovers your money mind-set.

If you want to read two books on money mind-set I suggest you read *The Energy of Money* by Maria Nemeth PhD which you will find challenging and *Coach Yourself to Wealth* by Shirley McKinnon.

I also suggest you read *The Money Tree* by Diana Mathew who managed to dig herself out from under a mountain of debt by first changing the way she thought about money.

And anything by money saving expert, Martin Lewis, is a must-read. Start with *MoneySavingExpert.com*

Melanie had to start by conquering the childish feelings that she was helpless and didn't understand money and her belief that someone else should take care of her money worries.

She had to change her victim mind-set. But as Melanie discovered, managing money becomes satisfying grown-ups work.

Take *The Money Chimp* Test

The better you understand *your* current money managing habits and skills the more likely you are to develop more resourceful habits and skills that lead to more positive results.

That's why I developed a test.

The Money Chimp is an inexpensive online test that takes about seven minutes to complete. You answer 35 questions and get back a personalised 20-page report of your money managing habits and skills with specific recommendations.

Here's the link: *www.moneychimp.net*

Yes, the test and report costs a small amount of money. But this test potentially can save you wasted time and a lot of money in the future.

People who have taken *The Money Chimp* test say:

"I am a financial planner and *The Money Chimp* test is bang on target. Brilliant."   **Ken**, Financial Advisor

"It was frighteningly accurate and gave me the big wake-up call I needed to sort out my finances."
                                Steven, Software designer

"The report described my money managing skills accurately and highlighted the blind spots with practical recommendations."
                                Eric, Life Skills trainer

"*The Money Chimp* report totally grabbed the attention of my 19 and 25 year olds."
                        Mark, Father of two young adults

"Me and my girlfriend loved the book. We both did the test and the book made so much more sense because we could relate our skills to each section. We have started applying what we learned."

                Tim and Sarah, Young couple 26 and 25

Let's now look at the top 10 money managing habits and skills.

The top 10
money managing principles

I conducted an extensive review of books, courses, websites and literature on money management. As I expected the key topics covered income, expenditure, assets and liabilities.

But I clearly identified five money managing habits - *earning, spending, saving, investing* and *giving*; and five money managing skills - *monitoring, focusing, reducing, developing* and *taking actio*n.

Money *champs* develop five good habits:

Habits

- **Earn** more than enough income to meet their needs.
- **Spend** less than they earn (and they know their liabilities)
- **Save** money (pay themselves 10% first, save for emergencies, plan for the future)
- **Invest** (they create assets, pensions, property etc).
- **Give** money to reputable charities.

And they develop five good skills. They:

Skills

- **Monitor** their income and expenditure and savings and investments.
- **Focus** and have clear financial plans
- **Reduce** wasteful, superfluous or unnecessary spending and expenses.
- **Develop** their money managing skills and financial literacy. And they;
- **Take action and apply** what they know.

Money *chumps* who struggle with money make these Top 10 mistakes:

- **Not earning enough** (when you can earn more).
- **Spending more than you earn** and wasting money. This also includes spending 'borrowed' money you can't repay and racking up huge credit card debts.
- **Not saving any money** for emergencies, holidays, Christmas gifts etc.
- **Not investing money** wisely or at all.
- **Not giving**.
- **Not monitoring** what you earn, spend, save, invest or give.
- **Not focusing on financial goals or targets.**
- **Not reducing** expenditure when it's obvious that's what's needed
- **Not developing** your money managing skills or financial literacy.
- **Not applying** what you are learning.

Time to review

I suggest you reread the top 10 money managing principles. Which of the habits and skills sound *most* like you? What are you already doing well and where do you need the most help?

And what are you learning so far? What's making sense? What key insights are you getting about the way you manage money so far?

If you implement even a small amount of the recommendations in this book you should start to see an improvement in your personal finances and your ability to manage your money.

So I'm now going to explore each of the five habits and five skills in more detail and give you some practical ideas to try out. These practical ideas genuinely work, but be warned, they will not work if you don't try them.

So we'll start by exploring the five money managing habits.

Part 3

The Five
Money Managing Habits

Habit #1 Earning

The reality is most people *do* earn enough money. But most people spend more than they earn on monthly fixed and variable expenses. We use the *monthly* time period because that's how most debt advisors and banks assess your ability to manage money and repay loans.

Even if you don't have a loan, start thinking how much it costs you to live - on average - *per calendar month*. We will soon explore what you typically spend your money on each month.

For now, on average, how much money do you *earn* every month?

'Earnings' is another name for income. Importantly, if you are an employee and wage earner, you need to know your exact take-home pay, *after-tax* (income).

Ask your boss or pay manager to provide you with a pay advice slip which will show all earnings and any regular or periodic deductions including tax, union fees, pension contributions etc.

In addition to knowing how much you earn each month, it's important to know the *source* of that money.

Three sources of income

The tax department segments income into three key sources:

- **Earned income** - salaries or self-employed income
- **Non-earned income** - pensions, benefits, dividends and annuities, bank interest, reimbursements
- **Other sources of income** - winnings, gifts etc.

So the tip here is to start identifying the source of your income.

If you earn a wage, the source of income is typically *earned income*. If you receive bank interest that's deemed *non-earned income* – but its still income. If you win £1,000 on the lottery, technically you have to declare that as income and pay tax on it. But it would come under *other* income.

Sometimes I get asked about *reimbursements*. Let's say your boss asks you to buy coffees for the team and you pay for it with your cash or credit card.

Or say you use a company car for a work related purpose and need to refuel that vehicle but you pay for the fuel on your credit card. Well you want to be reimbursed, right?

Your employer will reimburse the amount back to you but they usually ask for a receipt to reimburse the correct sum. So whenever you purchase anything on the job, *get a receipt!* And give it to your employer so you can be reimbursed immediately.

Obviously you wouldn't need to declare that as a source of income because you've already earned and paid tax on that money. So you don't want to pay tax twice.

However, if you are self-employed you might be required to show *all* expenses *and reimbursements* in your bookkeeping and maybe even on invoices.

The best advice is to talk to an accountant or book keeper.

Earn more than 'just enough'

Your goal isn't to earn just *enough* money to cover just your monthly living expenses. Your goal is to do better than that! The goal is to create surplus cash.

Most people are about two or three pay days from financial trouble and about two to three months from chronic debt, serious money hassles and even personal bankruptcy (RBS 2012).

Crisis, the UK charity says some independent young adults are one month away from homelessness! That might be a bit dramatic but having volunteered for several years at their annual *Crisis at Christmas* event and heard the stories I am sad to say it can be a likelihood for some.

So here are three goals:

- Your first goal is to work out how much you earn per calendar month.

- Then you need to add up your expenses - what you spend, on average, on monthly bills and see if you have *more money than month* or *more month than money*. It may take you several weeks to work out your total average monthly commitments.

- Next, you should start setting aside some money for unexpected bills and financial emergencies (see Spending).

Carol had to pay a $2,000 veterinary bill and that money had to come from somewhere. Fortunately, she had set money aside for such emergencies.

But most people have *nothing* set aside for even a small emergency such as an unexpected car repair or a dental bill.

She went back over the last 24 months and reviewed all the *unexpected* bills she paid. She worked out that she needed about $3,000 in cash reserves – to be safe – just to cover 'unexpected' stuff.

Carol sets aside $60 a week in her *emergency fund*. Some years she doesn't spend anywhere near $3,000 on emergencies but it's there just in case.

As it turns out $3,000/£2,000 is about the right amount for most people.

The next goal is a biggie.

Have at least three months worth of monthly living expenses in cash reserves

I injured my back and was off work for three weeks with no pay. And it took another 10 weeks before I was back working full time. But I had saved up six months worth of living expenses and that's how we got through those 13 weeks.

Let's pretend your living expenses are £2,000 PCM. That means you'd need to save up £6,000. The best way to do this is to create a special bank account just for your *cash reserve fund*. Finally:

You need to save for the future and for special projects such as education or your retirement

How much do you need to save? Well, it depends.

Jillian wanted to attend a 12-month course. The fees were £7,500. She started saving two years before the course so when she enrolled she was able to pay in cash. But it got better. Because she was a cash up-front student they offered her a 20% cash discount of £1,500.

Bill has a Pension Scheme and for every $1,000 he wants back in retirement per annum he is contributing $10,000. His goal is to have a $40,000 a year pension so he will need about $400,000 in the scheme.

You need very clear *Earning* goals based on your current living expenses. And I'm advising you to earn enough to cover inevitable financial emergencies.

If you don't have *Earning* goals you will earn money, pay your bills and spend whatever is left over on right-here-right-now stuff. Usually fun stuff.

But we know most people over-spend.

There's wisdom in the old saying "Save for a rainy day!"

Most people who do my workshops learn to earn more, spend less, save more, set aside money for rainy days and reduce their debts.

But how can you earn more? Here's some ideas:

- **Ask for a pay rise.** Most people are due a pay rise but never ask for one. An employer is *not* obliged to offer you a pay rise if you don't ask. The key to a pay rise is to be of more value. Most people don't understand this. They arrive late, watch the clock and go home early if they can. Doing the opposite makes you more valuable.

  I often ask employees who they work for and they name their company or their boss. The reality is you actually work for yourself. You just happen to have one customer - your boss.

  Think of yourself as an *intrapreneur* running your own business *inside* someone else's business. Your job is to be of more value at work.

- **Work extra shifts or better paying shifts.** You might need to sacrifice your social life for a while. Nikola worked the night shift for two years and saved up to afford a 15% deposit on a small flat.

- **Work a second job.** Craig worked a four-hour shift at his local pub two nights a week but that money built up over time and he was able to clear his credit card debt over several months.

- **Sell stuff you don't use anymore.** A drummer from a rock band sold off three drum kits that were gathering dust in his loft. Fans bought those kits as 'collectibles'. And he cleared his credit card debts. Win-win!

  A 16 year-old sold his old *X-Box* and *PlayStation* games on *eBay*. Then he started selling other people's games for a small commission.

- **Start your own part-time business.** Young Jake was 17 and unemployed. The best he could manage was casual work at a local fast food for $4.27 an hour. He borrowed his dad's leaf blower and a rake and offered to clean front yards of small terrace houses in his neighbourhood.

  Most houses were within 300 yards from his own home. He charged $5 for a quick cleanup and he could do three houses an hour. Pretty soon he was making $15 an hour. That's significantly more than he was earning working in a fast food store. This is a kid with a profitable service business with most customers all within a short walk from home.

  Debbie has two kids and after work she irons. She used to sit and watch TV. Now she irons and makes extra money while she watches TV. That little business started from a letter box drop in her street.

  Lois is a touch typist who transcribes MP3s for legal firms. That gives her an extra £200 a week.

- **Get a better job.** Ironically, if you are of more value in your current job you can easily justify a pay-rise but sometimes you simply need to find a better job that pays more money.

Of course, do not do anything illegal like not declaring extra income especially if it is a cash-only business. It infers that the purpose of that business is to avoid paying tax. Keep impeccable records and seek qualified accounting advice.

Your greatest tool is to *think*.

What can I do to increase my income? Get creative. Like Debbie, start in your own street. Russell Conwell's book *Acres of Diamonds* claims there is probably more than enough money to be made close by to where you live if you look.

One final word. If you are an employee on a fixed income getting your finances under control will depend on *spending less* of what you earn and trying to *save more*. The creative way forward is to increase your earnings.

Remember Melanie who had £9,000 in credit card debts? There's no way on her wage she could have got out from under that debt by only spending less. It was only possible by taking on an extra job. Once her debt was cleared she quit that job and by then she was much better at managing her money.

Despite having a demanding job as a teacher a friend devoted four years to paying off his student loan by working a second job.

The couple who owed over £41,000 had to make drastic changes – cutbacks, downsizing, eliminating all luxuries such as dining out, taking second jobs, renegotiating gas and electricity rates etc.

That took a lot of discipline, sacrifice and willpower but after 22 months they were finally debt-free.

Sean was self-employed running a small cleaning company. He was able to pay off debts by selling more of his cleaning services and working longer hours for a time. But he increased his income and traded out of his debt.

I once had a $25,000 loan which I traded out of through hard work and some refinancing.

It is possible to be debt-free but it usually takes smart thinking and hard work. If you are frightened of hard work you will find it harder to be debt-free let alone financially free.

Another way to have more money might be to ask anyone who's borrowed money from you to repay it. Many people attending the workshop said that people owed them money. One young woman was owed £2,000 from a family member.

You can also increase your income through investing. Investments often can make more money faster than you can by working harder. But more on that later.

Your turn

It's time to review what you read and convert that into action steps.

- How much money do you actually earn?
- Find out where your income comes from (earned, non-earned, other)?
- What can you do increase your income?
- Re-read this chapter and brainstorm some ideas that would be easy for you to implement straight away.

Habit #2: Spending

The chief economist of the Royal Bank of Scotland (2012) suggested that most people spend 130% of their weekly income. This means that most of us are living beyond our means. And this is especially true of young people (18-25 year olds).

That extra money has to come from somewhere: usually your credit card and personal loans.

But what are you spending that extra money on? Do you remember the section on *infographics*? Did you *Google* what householders in your country spend money on? Here's a reminder.

Well firstly there's bills – taxes, rent, loans, weekly food shopping, transport, rates, utilities etc – what we call *grudge purchases*. Petrol is a grudge purchase because we *hate* spending money on it. Gas and electricity are grudge purchases. You don't ever get excited and yell, 'Yippee' when you pay your electricity bill.

Bills aside, the research suggests we waste money on stuff we don't need like beauty treatments, shoes, clothes, alcohol, cigarettes, entertaining, gadgets - consumer goods that lose value as soon as you leave the shop.

We also get charged for 'hidden' expenses such as bank fees, charges and interest. By the way, they are not actually hidden at all but in plain view if you read your bank statements carefully!

You cannot avoid spending money but you need to ensure that your spending does not exceed your income.

That's why you need to know your current living expenses almost down to the penny. Living expenses means what it costs you just to live, on average per calendar month (PCM).

Most people have a *general* idea but some people have no idea at all. You need to work this out.

Your main monthly expenses typically segment into:

- **Liabilities** – rent, mortgage, personal loans

- **Recurring bills** – rates, insurances, school fees

- **Periodic bills** – gas, electricity, water, rates etc

- **Consumer debt** – loans, credit cards and charge card payments, fees and interest charges

- **Living expenses** – food, household spending, transport, etc

- **Discretionary spending** - *fun money*. Fun money is the most wasteful. Your money disappears on simple pleasures like coffees, takeaways, dining out, social events, holidays, fashion, gadgets and gifts.

You can certainly reduce your spending in any of these categories but for a quick result start to focus on reducing *discretionary spending*.

Here's an example. Ian complains he doesn't have enough money. But he smokes. His brand costs £9.32 and he smokes five packets a week. Over a year that's £2,432.20. Ian clearly *has* enough money to spend on cigarettes!

But does £2,432.20 seem a lot to you? It does to me and I can't see the point of what seems to me like 'burning' money *and* harming your health. Ian takes home about £25,000 a year after-tax so £2,432 is almost 10% of his take-home income!

Steven monitored what he spent on alcohol. Turns out he spends about £180 every Friday night. That's about £9,360 on alcohol a year. Steven also complains of not having *enough* money. But he clearly has enough money to spend on alcohol.

Kirsty's mobile phone plan is $35 per month ($420pa) but she loves downloading music and streaming movies and videos so her actual monthly phone bill always carries an *excess charge* and bumps it closer to $67 per month ($804). That's almost double - an additional $384.

These young people complain they haven't got enough money to pay their bills but they have got enough to spend on treats and luxuries.

Let's say you smoke, drink *and* overuse your mobile phone. Using the above figures that's GBP£12,596 (USD$19,399 and AUD$26,261.) That's a fair chunk of change! In the UK, US *and* Australia that's enough money for a deposit on a small apartment!

And let's say you need £2,000 PCM living expenses. That's six months worth of living expenses in cash reserves, right there. The reality is most people probably have *enough money* but are wasting it on stuff that doesn't matter, or worse, stuff that damages their health.

But what else can you do with that money?

Well I'm going to argue, pay down your debt; or invest that money in a pension scheme; or go back to university and get a qualification; or start a business.

Anything but do something much better with that money! Otherwise it's a sad waste. By the way, I am sure tobacco, alcohol and mobile phone companies really appreciate your lack of discipline.

Start to identify *exactly* what you spend your money on each month. Get a notebook and write down *everything* you spend. Or use a spreadsheet.

There are also some good Apps for your phone like *Expense Tracker* or *Pocket Expense* that track expenses and even send you alerts if you are nudging towards breaking the budget. But I've noticed that people learn more about managing money from using the good old pen, paper and calculator.

UK money saving expert, Martin Lewis suggests that a key benefit is once you start tracking your spending you can start making savings. He says that 70% of consumers can make significant savings on their phone, internet, utility and energy bills simply by shopping around and switching suppliers.

Lewis says two big lessons you need to learn are that suppliers are in business to make money. He says most customers pay dearly for their loyalty by not shopping around especially on things like energy and phone and internet bills and even bank loans.

But you can't make any savings unless you know your current plan or tariff, your usage and what you spend on average each month, quarter and year. Most people just don't know. Or bother to find out.

So the big recommendation is to ...

Get receipts for everything and read your bank statements

Emily, is in her early 30s and she loves shopping. As an exercise she started collecting receipts. After two months she was stunned at how much she spent on coffees and lunches alone. When she cut down on those treats she was equally stunned at how fast she saved up for something of greater value such as a well-earned holiday. This month she is flying to India with her husband for their wedding anniversary, something they've dreamed of for several years.

You need to STOP spending everything you earn on frivolous, short-term treats and START setting aside money for lasting rewards such as a home deposit or a well-earned holiday.

The goal is to *earn more*, *save more* and *spend less than you earn*. Remember: most Brits spend 130% of their weekly income!

Not so obvious are debt transactions such as credit cards, store cards, loans, borrowings, fees, charges and penalties.

Maybe in the past, banks targeted young people because they racked up huge credit card debts ever so quickly. But banks have discovered while it's easy to lend money the trick is getting it back. Banks are concerned if you fall over the edge into a cycle of *unpayable debt.*

I already mentioned Steven who spends an average of £180 on alcohol every Friday night. That's nearly £800 a month! He pays for those drinks on his credit card. And he rarely pays off his credit card on time so he gets hit with late fees and interest charges.

Alcohol is so wasteful. It's expensive. You drink it. An hour later you pee it out. And the next day you have a hangover. And we call that fun!

Most people do not pay off their entire end-of-month credit card bill on time – or even the interest only component – so they start getting interest on interest (and this is an example of money making more money *for the banks.*)

Worse yet, some young people do not realise they are even paying interest on interest payments as soon as they miss a payment! Time goes so fast and over 12 months you would be staggered at what you've paid in interest alone.

I said earlier that interest payments are *hiddens* but in fact they are not hidden at all. They are in plain sight on your bank statements. But they will remain *hidden* if you don't bother to read your bank statements. So learn to read statements. Read the bit that says: *Interest Paid This Month.*

Ask for receipts and always cross-check those receipts against the statements.

I once bought an item for $136 but the credit card statement showed I was charged $316. I hadn't even looked at the receipt issued at the point of sale and didn't pick up this error until over a month later.

After a trip to the States I discovered someone in Arizona had purchased a $1,299 laptop on my credit card. Fortunately, I check my statements and the bank reimbursed that fraudulent purchase.

Your main job is to get rid of credit card and store card debt. Do whatever you can to reduce and clear any card debts and then use your card responsibly.

The big killer can be store cards as they carry heftier APR interest fees. This is why big department stores encourage you to sign up to their loyalty card. Store cards are, of course, okay if you pay them off on time.

Our drummer didn't realise that one of his store cards was incurring 27% interest PCM. If he missed the payment he was paying 27% on the 27%!

Once he started reading every statement carefully he started picking up details like fees, fines and interest charges and even overcharges.

The other money trap is your mobile phone. According to a major phone company, young women rack up massive bills on talk time, downloads and bandwidth usage that exceeds their monthly phone plan.

I was on a train from London to Edinburgh and over-heard a young girl chatting about new shoes she had purchased. That conversation lasted all the way from Paddington to Peterborough! Maybe she had a generous phone plan, but charges hike once you exceed the usage allowance.

Another trap for young women is the exorbitant amount they spend on shoes (they wear once) and clothes (they wear two to three times) and cosmetics and beauty products and treatments.

The biggest money pit is dining out. Emily was spending a whopping £1,200 *a month* on meeting friends for coffee and lunch.

A study showed that young city workers spend around £50 a week on coffee and snacks. That's up to £2,600 a year. But if you throw in newspapers, magazines and taxis that balloons out to around £112 per week - or £5,824 a year. Of course, if you include the cost of a weekly 'quick drink' after work this can nudge closer to £10,000 a year, as Steven discovered.

But even if you eat at home look at how money is wasted. Did you know that most Brits throw away 60% of fresh food such as bread, fruit, vegetables that they purchase each week from the supermarket? *That's 60p per every £1.*

And most people never identify how much they spend on the treats included in their weekly shop. For example, chocolate, biscuits, soft drink, crisps etc.

OK, here are some small but important steps forward:

- From now on ask for receipts for everything you purchase. Everything.
- Buy 12 big freezer bags. (I buy those sturdy zip lock freezer bags).
- Label them January, February, March etc and then each month START putting *all* your receipts – month by month - inside the appropriately labelled bags.
- In addition print out every monthly statement – bank, credit card, store card statements and put them in the bags as well.
- Read the statements carefully. Go line by line with a ruler and a red pen. A friend of mine discovered he was still being charged £35 per month for a gym membership he thought had cancelled two years prior!
- Use Apps like *Expense Tracker*, *Xpenditure* or *iSpending* to monitor your spending.
- You can use your phone to take a photo of the receipt and send that back to your computer.
- Learn to use a spreadsheet and sort expenses into categories to see what you spend your money on and per category.

Your bank may even have a free downloadable spreadsheet and there are hundreds of free online expense ledgers and Apps available.

In any case, you have to start seeing what you spend your hard-earned money on.

Please do not ever say, "I don't want to do this because I am scared at what I might find." This is head-in-the-sand denial!

The point is to get information. You need to know your average expenses, and to do that you will need more than one month's expenses.

The group of young people who attended the money managing workshop collected all their expenses over 12 weeks. Once they got into the new habit of collecting receipts, printing out statements and checking they were – at first - shocked at what they wasted money on. But soon they started to see spending patterns.

Importantly, look for surprises in your expenses. Look at your bank statements and receipts and the items your purchased and ask yourself how you ended up making that purchase. Was it on a whim or a impulse? For example, you popped out to buy bread and milk and came home with a new outfit!

Doing this activity will help you become aware of your spending behaviour patterns and help you make better choices.

Lisa spent £400 a month on average on clothing.

She said, "How can that be? It's only £15 here and £25 there." But it all adds up! But note her insight was that it was *per month* meaning it had become a habit.

By the way, *Skill #1 Monitoring* is very much connected to *Skill #2 Focusing*. Once you start closely monitoring your spending you can start setting targets for spending and reducing unnecessary expenses.

Lisa still likes buying new clothes but she has reduced that to around £100 per month. She used the other £300 per month she spent on clothes to pay off her credit card debt, which now stays at zero.

You should carefully review expenses like utilities such as gas and electricity. You might discover you are paying too much. Or it could mean the way you use gas and electricity is expensive.

Did you know you can usually negotiate a better rate at any time? A short phone call to your supplier could result in reduced bills.

Most utility companies base the rate on the number of rooms. My wife and I are *empty nesters*. We don't stay up late or run loads of appliances or run the heating excessively. I was able to reduce my gas and electricity bill by 12% because I asked! I saved £289 pa. That may not sound much as the saying goes, 'Every little helps'.

The same principles apply at the business level.

A company had revenues of $1m and overheads of $900,000 per annum. That leaves $100,000 net profit.

They listed all overheads from most expensive down to the cheapest. They took the top five expenses and were able to negotiate 5% off those top five bills. That's $45,000! That $45,000 saving is nearly a 50% increase in profits.

Collect receipts, read statements, phone suppliers – do anything to get a much clearer picture of how you spend money each month.

Remember Steven? He dramatically reduced his entertainment costs. "First, I stopped buying rounds of drinks for mates. I still spend about £60-80 a week at the bar but I now clear my credit card bill at the end of every month."

Smart money expert, Carl Richards, says people spend so little time thinking about how they spend money. Reading bank statements and thinking about what you purchased and why is a great habit that will make you much better at managing your money.

Most wealth coaches suggest you allocate at least one hour a week to managing money activities such as reading statements and receipts. They'll ask you to get a notebook and identify the categories you spend money on, too.

Recently I did a magazine quiz on *'What type of spender are you?'.* Nine questions reveal five types of spender - *Careful, Bargain Hunter, Self Gifter, Retail Therapy* and *Compulsive Shopper*.

You've probably guessed that I came out as a *Careful Spender.*

Quizzes can be fun but if it makes you more aware of your spending habits then it's valuable.

As you will discover awareness is the key to money mastery.

Your turn

- Do you know how much you spend each week, month, quarter, year? Using ideas in this chapter, what could you start doing to get a clearer picture of your spending?
- Review the seven categories again on page 91 and see if you have a gut feel for where you spend the most money?
- Focus on discretionary spending. Where are you *obviously* wasting money? What do you need to STOP spending money on?

Habit #3: Saving

There is nothing better than the feeling of knowing you have money set aside as savings.

The most cited basic wealth advice is: Save 10% of what you earn. If you are a wage earner, that means 10% of your *after-tax,* take-home pay. Let's say you earn £100 per week, after-tax. You save £10 a week. It doesn't sound much but some people have no savings.

Josey has been saving 10% of everything she has earned since she was 14 years old. She had saved over £15,000. She has always had *enough* money in the bank and a sense of security.

Our drummer EARNS a LOT but SPENDS more than he earns and saves NOTHING. And even after several years of being a highly paid session player he still has nothing to show for his efforts. He confronted that reality in the money-managing workshop.

By contrast, a mate of mine was in a successful rock band and despite the temptation of a wild lifestyle, lived modestly and channelled his earnings into savings and property.

After a few years when the band's fame faded he was the only band member with something to show for their success. He still receives about $5,000 a year for music/performance royalties but he says, "I'm so glad I put money away at the time and then invested. I now own several properties that give me a comfortable post-rock star lifestyle."

Most pop stars and sports stars shine for *about* four years and very few have an enduring career. You may remember Shakin' Stevens from the 1970s? He knew that he wouldn't always be a pop star. I believe 40 years on, his property portfolio gives him a comfortable lifestyle because he saved money and invested wisely.

As a boy, Paul McCartney lived in a council house in Liverpool so knew the value of saving and living within his means. He bought properties near the Abbey Road Studios and still has the home he bought in St John's Wood in the 1960s. If you walk past the house you can see the famous bathroom window that *she* came in through.

Apparently, Ringo Starr still owns the shops he bought in Chelsea in the mid 60s'.

And I believe Mick Jagger's grand kids live in the properties he bought in Chelsea with earnings from his early days with the *Rolling Stones*. In those days Chelsea wasn't a prestigious suburb but reportedly Jagger has done very nicely from property, and it appears he *can* get satisfaction. Despite his notoriety, it seems he was really just a hard working lad who knew the value of saving and quietly investing.

Michael Palin and Terry Gilliam of *Monty Python* fame are both on record for living well within their means. Even though at one point they were part of a famous comedy team they controlled their spending and invested well.

All these performers followed the pattern of making money at the height of fame and saving and investing for the future.

Even if you're not a pop star, save at least 10% of what you earn. When your funds reach a certain level, invest in something that pays a good rate of interest like an ISA or tax-free pension.

My son saved up enough money to buy shares in his 20s. Save and invest. Save 10% and don't touch it unless you are ready to invest in shares, property or business. An investment usually makes money faster than you could earn it over time.

As I discovered there is no point amassing savings and earning a piddling .001% in a bank account. A friend invested $10,000 in shares and over six years turned that into $40,000. Had he left that money in the bank it would have earned $18! He sought good advice and you should too.

If you can't save 10% save 5% but save *something* and don't ever spend it. Pretend that account doesn't exist. Some people say they *can't* save. But I hope you're discovering, that's not true.

Everyone can save something. I have seen 18 year olds put £25 a week into an ISA. A year later they have been saving money in a tax-free environment that has earned good interest.

When we first moved from Australia to the UK in 2009 I saved £11,000 over two years. That money came from earnings, doing extra income projects and even selling off unwanted stuff like a psychology book from my university days that sold for £65.

Troy sold a jet ski, a kayak, snow skis and diving gear that was gathering dust in his garage. That money cleared his credit card debt and paid off a huge chunk of his personal loan. As a result the loan period and repayments were significantly reduced.

OK, here's what works and what I recommend. It can be a tough call but its doable.

- Save 10% of your after-tax, take-home pay. Don't *ever* touch it unless it is being channelled into a sound investment like an ISA or property.

- Save at least £2,000 for unexpected bills and financial emergencies. You need a safety net and an emergency fund is a form of insurance.

- Start to save at least 3-6 months of average monthly living expenses to create a financial buffer. You need cash reserves.

  The focus here is protection and peace of mind.

Most financial stress is the result of knowing you have zero financial buffer or cash reserves.

- Start saving for future projects such as your education, or a house deposit or retirement.

- Save to invest. (Obviously get qualified advice.)

Once you start to see results you will be encouraged to continue the savings habit.

Most money experts recommend 'paying yourself first' by saving at least 10% of your take-home pay. They suggest never spending it unless you are investing it into something that is tax efficient and earns you a lot more than bank interest. (Make sure you seek advice from someone like a financial planner.)

In reality, saving 10% is probably not enough anymore, but it is still the best starting point for creating the savings habit.

Diane and I *still* save 10% of everything we earn and apart from a small mortgage we have no debts. We actually live well on less than 60% of our after-tax income. At our stage in life we do not have the money worries that plague many people our age.

And this can be true for you, too, once you get the savings habit.

But here's the problem: most people pay their bills, do their shopping, and splash a little cash *and then* they try and save 10% from whatever is left over, which is usually 10% of very little or nothing.

So start by saving 10% of your after-tax income *first* and then spend. Pay yourself first.

In any case good money managers save a set amount *before* they pay their bills, go shopping or splash some cash.

The four most important savings goals are:

- SAVE money for financial emergencies.
- SAVE at least three months of living expenses.
- SAVE for investment goals.
- SAVE for retirement.

But there's just one problem with being a good saver.

Warning: You are not an ATM or an interest-free bank

Here's a big heads up.

Trust me, once you get into the habit of saving you will become a magnet *for people who don't save* - usually family and friends. And once you have money it seems the letters *ATM* magically appear like a huge neon sign over your head.

Lisa is a good saver but her brother isn't. He is always 'borrowing' money from her and he expects to borrow money because he's 'family'. And in their family it's considered selfish to refuse to help.

Under those conditions her saving plans repeatedly fell by the wayside.

Her brother cleaned her out of the £2,000 she had saved up to pay off a credit card bill. While he said he was 'borrowing' the money, two years later she is yet to see any of that money repaid.

So if you are a good saver, keep it quiet.

Lisa felt guilty for having money *and her brother knew how to make her feel guilty.* Saying 'No' felt like a betrayal. Her brother Jason pouted and yelled and got angry. He just *had to* have the latest *X-Box*. And new trainers. He even begged and pleaded her to help him pay his rent!

Lisa felt responsible for Jason and it took some convincing for her to realise she was actually being *irresponsible* by continually bailing him out.

Lisa no longer lends money to Jason.

She saved up for a deposit on a small apartment in outer London and three years later the value has increased enough for her to finance her second apartment and rent the first! That may not be your goal but for Lisa that has been a massive breakthrough in her relationship with money and realisation of a dream!

Get the facts first

Any wealth coach will ask you to make a full list of what you spend money on and then actively look for ways to reduce your spending so you can make savings. But that won't happen without the facts.

A London-based programmer was ignoring the poor state of his finances and was even scared to do the ideas suggested in this book.

After four months of getting a much clearer picture of his finances he made a very bold move. He found a better paid job in Manchester where the rent and the cost of living wasn't as steep as London.

A year later he had cleared his credit card debt and had saved for a deposit on his own apartment.

"I was being irresponsible with money. I was actually frightened to look. But once I got clear on my finances I made better decisions and life started to improve rapidly. Changing jobs and cities wasn't easy and I'll probably move back to London eventually but for now I'm saving money and getting ahead faster than I ever thought possible."

Here's a very smart tip. Most people get the idea about cutting back to save money. But they cut back on little things like coffees and lunches.

But you should definitely look at bigger expenses such as your energy bills. You might renegotiate your tariff and that can translate into significant savings *and* then you can keep treating yourself to coffee treats.

They say, "Look after the pennies and the pounds will take care of themselves." But you can be penny wise and pound foolish, too.

Ultimately, getting a clearer picture of how you spend your money will lead to better choices and savings.

Your turn

- Are you good at saving money?
- Do you pay yourself first?
- Will you save at least 10% of your after-tax, take-home pay?
- Will you create a special savings account just for your 10% savings?
- Can you work out what three months worth of living expenses add up to?
- How much money are you going to save in an emergency fund?
- Do you need to create a Christmas fund?
- What's starting to make sense to you?
- Getting any ideas for action?

Habit #4: Investing

The number #1 advice given by all experts is: *Spend less than you earn.* And this should allow you to save.

I've suggested you to save at least three months of living expenses, save for financial emergencies and use surplus cash to reduce debt. But the best reason for saving is to enable you to start investing.

Investing is the proven route to financial freedom because usually your investments increase in value much faster than your ability to earn the same amount of money over the same period of time.

Investing usually involves borrowing money and therefore going into debt.

As mentioned, there is *good debt* and *bad debt*. *Good debt* is borrowing money to purchase something that *grows* in value such as a property. Bad debt is borrowing money for something that *loses* value.

Best-selling *Rich Dad, Poor Dad* author, Robert Kiyosaki suggests investing in tax deductible, income generating assets is the best form of *good debt*.

Your investments should provide you with an income, a dividend, growth or a healthy return if and when you sell.

The four main investment strategies are *property, shares, cash* and *businesses.*

Residential Property

In the 1980s, my wife, Diane and I saved up $7,000 for a deposit and borrowed $11,000 and purchased a small $18,000 residential property in Australia.

We spent another $12,000 fixing it up and four years later we sold that property for $65,000 with a profit of $54,000 (after paying for legal fees and stamp duty). We could never have saved $54,000 in four years!

We were *20-something* parents with a young family and it was our first home. And notice it was a *small* property and a small loan. But that's how we got on the property ladder.

Plus we did most of the renovation work ourselves. To this day I know how to plaster, paint, fix electrics, tile, grout, replace glass and a host of other handyman skills. And Diane is very handy with a paint roller.

Now, I am not advising you to invest in property. But we feel comfortable with residential property and it's always been good for us for two reasons.

Firstly, every property we've bought increased in value and therefore the equity we acquired when we sold.

Secondly, the increase in equity allowed us to buy a much nicer family home for $90,000 - also with a mortgage. But as we saved and paid down the debt, we were then able to release equity from the property and invest in rental property.

Property was an obvious investment choice for most people because you need somewhere to live and it is usually better to be paying off the mortgage on your own home than renting and paying off someone else's mortgage.

Rental Property

If you have a mortgage and live in that home, your home is actually considered a *liability* because it *costs* you money.

However, if you *don't* live in it yourself and earn rental income it's deemed an asset because it *makes* you money.

Fred, a nurse with the NHS bought a small house in Bristol, but transferred to a hospital in Kent. Rather than sell his home, he decided to *rent out* his property in Bristol. The rental income not only pays his mortgage in Bristol but most of the rent on his flat in Kent as well!

How clever is that?

Karen and Ian live and work in Reading but bought a small rental apartment in London which has already gone up in value. They are now intending to borrow against their London flat to buy *another* small flat.

Rental property is exciting because you are earning income from the property, your tenants are paying off your mortgage, you are getting the increase in value and you can borrow against the equity to buy more property.

Property investment specialists like Vicki Wusche or Steve Bolton teach investors how to achieve financial independence through investing in low cost, rental property. Steve wrote *Successful Property Investing* and his company *Platinum Property Partners* offers specific training in *Houses of Multiple Occupation* (HMOs).

I mentioned Mick Jagger earlier. One of his first goals when *The Stones* started to make money was to buy a house and stop paying rent. At the time he bought low cost property in the *undesirable* suburb of Chelsea!

Commercial Property

It doesn't have to be residential property. Malcolm bought a small industrial shed when he was 24 which turned into a lifetime love for commercial property. A bricklayer by trade, he specialises in building *off-the-plan* warehouses that earn him money before they are even built!

This section might sound like a advertisement for property, but property is just one investment strategy worth exploring.

Shares

Rob likes shares. He can't understand why anyone would lock their money up in bricks and mortar. He began share trading in university as a way of paying off his student loan. He developed a flair for doing the research needed to invest wisely in shares and has built an impressive portfolio in 'penny' shares over time.

Cash

Ian is a financial planner who specialises in working with very busy people who work hard and make a good income. Most of their money is tied up in a nice family home but they don't have spare *lifestyle cash*. Basically, they are asset rich and cash poor.

Ian's clients realise that turning 50 is a few short years away and they now realise they may not be able to fund their current lifestyle in their retirement once they stop working.

Ian helps them to put their cash to better use than, say, a lease on an expensive European car. As I understand it he unlocks equity in the family home and channels that money into high growth, tax-free environments like short-term ISAs and accessible pension schemes.

The good news is this is an investment strategy worth exploring for *any one* at *any age*. (Seek advice!)

Businesses

I personally love businesses. My first service business cost me $500 to start and within a year I had turned that into $32,000 profit. I love buying low and selling high and making money on the spread. I often encourage young people to start buying and reselling on *eBay*.

Don and Jeff teach people how to set up profitable *Fulfilled By Amazon (FBA)* businesses. They say a small investment in training and mentoring can turn into a six-figure business for the right person.

But which investment strategy is right for you?

Our 27-year old drummer said, "I'm focused on work, getting debt-free and saving money for a deposit on a flat." So maybe property resonates most with him.

In any case, start by educating yourself. Read books and attend courses. The most successful investors invest time and money *ongoing* in training, professional advice and support.

Right now, you might well be wasting your money with little to show for it long-term. But a year goes by very fast and five years even faster. One day you might realise you should have started investing a lot sooner.

Your turn

- Of the four main investment vehicles (property, shares, cash, businesses) which one sounds or feels right to you? Why?
- Pick one and do a web search, visit a library or go online to your bank and do some background reading.
- Are you starting to see the link between earning, saving and investing? What's going through your mind?
- Start playing money games like *Monopoly, Life* or *Cashflow.*

Habit #5: Giving

It is good to give. But what's happening here? I have just urged you to focus on saving and reducing your spending and now I'm saying give some of it away?

That's exactly what I am saying.

People who have their finances under control are generally more charitable. *Giving* means giving money to others with no expectation or requirement to be repaid.

Most people give money to charities or causes. Some people give money to a church. And most of us give money to family or friends as gifts or loans.

Giving works. It's actually good for you to give. We are hard wired to contribute and we feel bad when we can't help *or can help, but don't.*

Giving helps someone who is genuinely less fortunate than yourself. Usually they are living under adverse conditions unlikely to change for the better, anytime soon. But give wisely.

I used to give money to the homeless on the street but after volunteering with *Crisis at Christmas* I learned that the money is better *donated* to a reputable charity like *Crisis*, *Red Cross* or *Unicef* known for putting your donations to good use.

Crisis don't recommend giving money directly to the homeless or to beggars because rarely is it put to good use. For a while, in London, everywhere you went there were women from Eastern Europe begging with baby or a small child. Sadly, most of these beggars are the face of organised crime.

So only give to registered and reputable charities.

Yes, charities have operating costs but don't let that stop you from donating. Do your homework and find a charity you feel comfortable with because giving is good for others and giving fuels your drive for success.

Wealth coach, Sarano Kelley recommends donating 10% of your income to charities but if that seems a stretch start by donating your *time*.

I volunteer at the annual *Crisis at Christmas* programme in London and have learnt a lot about my own values and life goals by volunteering.

Make a commitment to choose a charity that you feel comfortable with and then help out. Being a volunteer offers a range of life affirming benefits for the charity, for you and their beneficiaries.

What about giving to family and friends?

I enjoy giving money to my children and give money to family and friends on special occasions such as birthdays. You might too. But avoid giving money to family or friends if its to supplement their income especially if they somehow make you feel guilty for saying 'No'. It is a bad habit to start.

If someone asks to *borrow* money, they are inferring they intend to *pay it back*. If they rarely pay you back they are taking advantage of your good nature. They are treating you like an interest-free bank and worse, if you are a soft touch, you are training them to be irresponsible.

If they ask you to *give* them money that's different. Giving is not *lending* money. And lending money is not a *gift*. But giving should never hurt the giver.

Remember Lisa? Her brother, Jason, 'borrowed' £2,000 from her and is yet to repay any of that money. She does it because he's family. And he rationalises that somehow she is obligated to help him because she is family.

Her mother says, "If you were stupid enough to give him money then you are a fool." So she gets no thanks or understanding for her generosity.

Lisa should have clearly established *'This is a loan that has to be repaid by <date>'.* That is the *only* reason I will *lend* you money. That's how banks work. It's *not* a gift. It's a loan.

Think about it this way. If her brother went to a bank what would they say? They would want collateral. In other words, what have you got worth £2,000 plus the fees to set up the loan and administer it, plus bank charges and interest if you miss the payments plus penalties if you default on the loan?

Lisa's brother is treating her like an unconditional, interest-free bank. But it's worse because he has no intention of repaying what he supposedly 'borrowed'.

And incredibly, he feels *entitled* to his sister's money!

Worse, every time Lisa 'lends' him money she is teaching him to be irresponsible. His thinking goes something like, "If I get into trouble, Lisa has cash."

What else could she have done?

She could have said, "This is a *gift*. You do not have to repay any of it." The problem is she needs the money herself and can't afford to give it anyway. And she wants Jason to repay the money.

So, be clear, it's *not* a gift.

She knows from long experience that whenever she 'lends' money to her brother, he will never repay money that she has worked hard to earn and something he is more than capable of doing himself.

Ironically, he resents the fact that Lisa *has* money to lend. A sense of entitlement will do that to you.

This is such a tough issue in a close-knit family where one person applies guilt-provoking and emotional pressure to get a 'free ride'. You have to resist the urge to be 'nice', helpful or a rescuer. (This dynamic is covered in detail in the book *The Energy of Money*.)

In my own extended family, there was a relative who spent all his parent's inheritance money, and then tried to borrow his sister's inheritance as well!

Family members will accuse you of being unfair but they are usually covering up issues they don't want to face such as they are being lazy or irresponsible.

And they *do* want a free ride. *Google* the *Free Rider Effect*. It is very well documented that the *free rider effect* can quickly lead to more serious problems.

I am a business coach and one of my clients, Peter, runs a successful agricultural irrigation supply company. Peter asked me to coach one of his young managers, Brian, who managed one of the stores located in a remote country region.

Brian seemed pleasant enough but I sensed something was wrong. He kept missing coaching appointments, cut sessions short and rarely did any of the activities we agreed on. And then there were things that didn't add up.

Eventually I told Brian he was wasting Peter's training budget and said I would recommend that Peter take a much closer look at Brian, the operation, the staff and the books.

Brian then confessed that he had racked up gambling debts and that he was stealing money from the company through pricing scams. Apparently, he would inflate the price of services, pocket a cash deposit and put the sale through the business at the correct cost with Peter none the wiser.

At this point, Peter said he would sack him and have him charged by the police. Brian pleaded and begged for a reprieve. He said he had two children to support and if he lost his job he'd lose his house. Peter still sacked him but took pity and *dropped the charges*.

Gradually, Peter discovered the full extent of Brian's scam. He had siphoned off over $235,000. Some months later, we heard he had done the *same* thing to his next employer only this time he was charged and jailed for three years.

Why have I included this story? Because Jason reminds me of Brian. Brian believed he was *entitled* to that money and was contemptuous of Peter's success.

Brian rationalised that Peter wouldn't miss it and didn't feel any remorse or responsibility for his actions and even blamed Peter for putting temptation in his way!

Peter and Lisa, both kind and compassionate people, had their heartstrings tugged and both went against their better judgment.

But people like Brian are only grateful for a short time and soon go back to their old habits. And people like Jason do not actually appreciate or value the compassion or generosity of others anyway.

The moral here is: *Giving should not hurt the giver.*

Diane and I have sponsored a child in Ethiopia for many years. This little girl will never be able to repay what we have invested into her future. However, our fulfilment has been immense.

A business colleague, Jeff, sponsors over 1,500 kids through his business. One of those kids grew up and eventually went to university and emerged with a political law degree and is now a major policy maker in Uganda. That young man has grown into a mature adult who is making a positive difference in his country. That would not have been possible without Jeff's sponsorship.

So the tips here are:

- It's good to give to others who are less fortunate.
- Giving shouldn't hurt the giver.
- It is not good to lend money to people who are more than capable of helping themselves.
- If it's a *loan* then you should ask to be repaid.

Finally, *give* thanks. We all have so much to be grateful for starting with the love and support of people in our lives. Be thankful that you *can* create the life you want. There actually *is* an abundance of opportunity if you just look.

But ultimately, aim to give back.

Your turn

- What do you feel about donating money to charities?
- Of all the charities you know which one appeals the most to you? Why that charity?
- Do a web search about the charity that interests you most?
- Make a list of people you lend money to? What have you learned about the people who borrow money from you? Especially what have you learned about people who don't repay their 'loans'?
- This week find a charity and donate £5. Notice how that feels.
- Cultivate an attitude of gratitude. What can you be grateful for today?

Part 4

The Five Money Managing Skills

Skill #1 Monitoring

For the next 30-90 days monitor your expenses. Write down *every* financial transaction. If you spend £1.50 on hot chips, write it down. If you spend £15 on a book, write it down. If you buy a $2 lottery ticket, write it down. If you spend $2.35 at the grocer on the way home, make a note of that as well. Track everything you spend for the next 30 days.

Ideally get receipts for everything. Everything.

You cannot and will not work out what money you need until you know how much money you spend each month down to the last penny. Good money managers know how much they spend.

Here's a fact: wealthy people monitor their money; poor people don't. That's one reason why poor people stay poor. You need to identify exactly how much you spend and what you spend it on. That data will help you set realistic targets and reduce your expenses.

Monitoring uses the skills of recording and analysing your spending using skills like *collating, data entry* and *reconciling*.

- **Collating** means collecting all receipts, bills and statements as mentioned. But it also means sorting that information into expense categories.

- **Data entry** means entering that information into a notebook, spreadsheet or ledger. Essentially you are showing money in and money out and by category (gas, rent, food shopping, school fees, train travel etc).

- **Reconciling** means cross checking the ledger against the actual bank statements and receipts so that everything matches and tallies and balances!

Once you start monitoring you might be shocked at what you discover. Most people will find their bank statements include bank interest, fees and charges automatically deducted from their account.

It stunned me to discover I was paying about $48 a month in late fees and interest charges on my credit card. That's nearly $500 a year! If you are not good at managing your money now, I guarantee this is happening!

But the good news is monitoring starts to pay off quickly.

I discovered I was still paying £35 a month for a gym membership I thought I had cancelled.

And I discovered I was still paying £5 per month for a online business membership I don't use. £60 a year isn't a lot but it's £60 I don't need to be spending.

Remember the girl who spent £400 a month on clothing? She didn't know it was that much until she started monitoring her spending.

Monitoring helps you realise how much you are spending and gives you choices.

Kevin was paying £1,836 PCM for a flat that wasn't that great. He found another flat that was smaller but of a better standard for £1,100 PCM. That's a saving of over £736 PCM or £8,832 a year.

Ian noticed the direct debit for energy bills increasing. He renegotiated his gas and electricity and saved £36 per month. That's over £432 a year.

When Ian checked his receipts he estimated he was spending nearly £10,000 a year on alcohol and nearly £2,432 on cigarettes. Combined, that's a 10% deposit on a small flat!

Lisa checked her mobile phone bills and usage. By changing her mobile phone plan and ditching streaming services she saved $32 a month. Ben's phone bills showed he was averaging £80 a month on downloads. That's £960 a year. He also jettisoned his internet plan and changed his phone habits. His phone bill now is a miniscule £10 a month.

Our drummer was shocked when he worked out how much extra debt he was incurring on his credit and store cards in late fees. "Doing the maths really motivated me to clear that debt! It was tough at first but I now manage my credit card – it doesn't manage me!"

You can't get savings like these without monitoring. Here's how I monitored my expenses for many years.

Start by getting 12 freezer bags and label them - January, February, March etc - one for each month of the year.

Start by putting any income statements or pay slips in the bag. For example last month I earned £3,874 and I spent £2,961. So I have a surplus of £913.

Put monthly bank statements and bills in the appropriate month-labelled bag. Include any amount that's set up as a direct debit or standing order to be automatically deducted from your bank account by a supplier such as gas, rent and rates.

Then start collecting receipts for everything. Train tickets, fuel, meals, food shopping. Everything. If you draw money out of an ATM put that receipt in the bag, too. If you can't get a receipt write the purchase down on a scrap of paper and put that note in the bag. To make reconciling easier collate the receipts in date order.

If you make a small petty cash purchase, include that too. For example, I bought a *Snickers* bar for a $1 at a petrol station. I wrote down the amount and the date on a piece of note paper and threw that in the bag.

At the end of the month get all your bank statements and all your receipts. Get a ruler and a highlighter and go down the list and match as many receipts as you can to the statements. You're trying to identify your total income and expenditure for each month.

Then you're going to sort out what you spend your money on into the categories I listed earlier - liabilities, recurring bills, periodic bills, consumer debt, living expenses and discretionary spending.

Years ago I did this manually in an exercise book with ruled columns. Nowadays I use a spreadsheet that shows amounts in columns labelled *date, description, amount, total* and *sub-totals per category* such as phone, rent, transport, meals, bank fees, postage, stationery, medical, insurances, pets, loans etc.

As an example, I know exactly how much we spend on train fares or food shopping every month and how much I spent on average each month over a year.

Interestingly, if you talk to a financial planner or a wealth coach they will want this detailed information, too.

OK, time to stop right here!

I know that some of my readers at this point are thinking, 'OCD alert'. I hate to say it but, yes, you need to be a little obsessive about this at first.

Remember Emily? It was her husband Patrick who asked her to get receipts for everything and tally them up at the end of the month. She felt he was prying *and* judging her. And she hated Patrick asking, "Did you get a receipt for lunch today?"

But getting receipts quickly became a habit. And then she saw that she was spending around £1,200 on lunches each month!

In my case, I was able to reduce my electricity bill by about £289 by monitoring expenditure over time and asking for a better rate. £289 doesn't sound much but combined with other savings it adds up. But now I'd rather spend that £289 on birthday or Christmas presents.

My brother, Pip, was able to reduce his energy bills by around £300 a year by renegotiating his tariff.

You'll discover that once you start monitoring, you want to track more! Melanie got into the swing of monitoring. She went through her credit card bill with a fine tooth comb and quickly realised that the bulk of her £9,000 debt was on beauty treatments, clothes, shoes, accessories and dining out.

Young people tell me it's too hard but when they do start monitoring they all say, "I wish I'd done this a lot sooner."

Monitoring lets you analyse your spending, but it allows you to forecast your future spending and start budgeting.

You might also rethink expensive habits. Steven no longer spends £180 a weekend on alcohol any more and Melanie rarely spends more than £100 a month on clothes now.

Without monitoring you just keep wasting money.

Your turn

- This week print out all your bank statements (deposit, loans, credit cards, store cards) and read them. Highlight any standing orders.
  Highlight all fees and charges. Importantly, check that you are not still paying for things you no longer use such as gym memberships.
- List every bill you receive and compile a list all your current suppliers like electricity, gas, rates, rent, insurance etc. You may need to do this over three–six months because some bills only appear quarterly or annually such as MOT or TV licence.
- Get 12 plastic freezer bags and label them for each month of the year.
- Start collecting receipts for everything you buy and put them into those bags.
- At the end of the month look at all the receipts you've collected. What are you noticing?
  Any insights about what you spend money on?
- Set up *mobile phone budget alerts* from your bank to monitor your spending.
- Last question: how is this book landing? Are you getting benefit? Is it making sense? Importantly, what have you decided to do as a result of what you've read so far?

Skill #2 Focusing

If monitoring is all about clearly identifying how you spend your money, focusing is all about identifying goals, targets and priorities.

You might want to reduce your credit card debt from £973 to zero. Or you might want to save up £1,400 for an overseas holiday. Or you might simply want to carry £100 spending money in your wallet to spend on movie tickets or dining out.

To improve your ability to manage money you need to have specific goals and priorities - *and focus on them.*

To set clear goals you need accurate information about your income and expenditure gathered in the monitoring stage. As you can see monitoring and focusing work together.

As far as money is concerned there are three targets to focus on:

- Targets to *increase* something (earn more)
- Targets to *decrease* something (spend less)
- Targets to *maintain* something (save more)

In any case your goals should be specific. You might set the target of saving £1,000 over the next 12 months to pay for next Christmas so you don't spend the next six months paying off a credit card debt.

Christmas credit card debt is the most common burden for many families in the USA, UK and Australia!

If you have monitored well, it is now a clear target for action. Having clear targets helps you make better decisions regarding what to do with your money.

Our drummer set the target of reducing his credit card debt from £7,000 to zero.

Remember the couple who racked up £41,000 in credit card debt? Well before they could reduce that debt they needed to know their income and their expenditure – *exactly*. Despite being dual income, highly paid professionals they discovered they were in a real mess. On average, they paid back £1,900 per month over the next two years.

Actually they played the *10% Debt Reduction Game*. Their first payment was £4,100; 10% of £41,000. That took the bill down to £36,900. Their next payment was £3,690 and so on. By month 22, the debt was down to £4,041 and they paid it off entirely. It was of course a little more with bank interest and charges, but you get the idea.

Their goal involved living frugally for a two years. They sold unwanted items, they took extra jobs, they stopped buying items they didn't need, they moved to cheaper accommodation. They took a 'whatever it takes' approach. And they worked closely with the bank to whittle that figure back to zero. Not everyone is that driven. *But it can be done.*

Author of *The Money Tree*, Diana Mathew was driving home from work and blacked out at the wheel of her new car. The accident left her with repair bills but she then discovered the car was uninsured!

She negotiated with the finance company to repay that debt but then a recession hit. She lost her job.

That lead to missed mortgage repayments and the bank moved to foreclose. By this stage she was $8,000 in debt and barely making ends meet and there was no possible way she would catch-up in the foreseeable future.

The first thing she did was list her debts and a realistic time frame to clear them. Then she divided her after-tax income into three groups. 10% went into a savings account, 20% was used to pay bills and reduce debts and she learned to live on the remaining 70%.

She listed *all* her liabilities and expenses. *Every* bill was scrutinised. She phoned every supplier and explained the situation and wherever possible a better rate was negotiated. Ironically, everyone was helpful. No one wanted to see her go under.

She got receipts for *everything* and analysed her spending patterns. She eliminated soft drinks, crisps, biscuits, cakes, coffees, take-aways – anything deemed a treat – from her weekly spend.

She said 'Let's *not* do lunch or coffee or drinks.' She took a packed lunch to work, cancelled the gym membership.

Standing orders for clubs and charities all got cancelled. She reduced or eliminated any superfluous loans and insurances.

She went on a financial witch-hunt for hidden fees and charges. She aimed to pay her credit card on time.

She got a new job and worked extra hours. She worked small part-time jobs.

She started reading everything she could on debt reduction and went to free courses that developed her personal finance skills and her relationship with money.

Four months later she was 100% debt free and had $2,000 in savings.

She even wrote a book called *The Money Tree* explaining how she did it.

The Money Tree has gone on to make her one of the best-selling personal finance authors in Australia and her simple 'get-out-of-debt' system has helped people worldwide.

At the heart of the book is the skill of monitoring. She could not have gotten this result without the facts. Monitoring and focusing enabled her to make some very smart choices with one goal: *to be debt-free as fast as possible.*

Getting out of debt must become a much higher priority than buying a new handbag, owning the latest 'smart' gadget or shouting your mates to an expensive round of drinks every Friday night.

Once out of debt you can set targets for improving your life like setting up an emergency fund, owning your own home or taking a well-earned holiday.

Your goal could be as simple as saving £300 per month for the next 25 years and retiring a millionaire!

Setting priority goals works closely with the skill of monitoring. As mentioned, performance falls into three categories. You must focus on:

- Things you need to STOP doing.
- Things you need to START doing.
- And things you need to CONTINUE doing (because its working).

Focusing is important because you are identifying specific things that need to change. Focusing allows you to decide where your money is better spent.

For example, spending money on alcohol could be better spent on reducing a credit card debt.

- **STOP** – stop spending so much on things that waste money such as cigarettes, alcohol, dining out, shoes, clothing, gaming, gambling.

- **START** – start doing things like reducing your credit card debts, saving for a holiday, or Christmas and birthdays, repaying a student loan faster.

- **CONTINUE** - continue with your savings plan.

Focusing requires accurate information. And that means you need to carefully monitor, track and analyse what you earn and spend. Only then can you make informed choices. There is no point setting a savings goal if you don't know where you currently waste money.

Remember the guy who moved from a flat of £1,836 a month to a flat for £1,100? Reducing expenditure to save money had to become a priority. To do that he had to move out of the city. The train fare went up by £200 per month but that was still £500 cheaper than where he was living. By the way expenses like rates also dropped accordingly.

It sounds simple but it isn't easy which is why most people don't get the results they need. It takes clear thinking and discipline. Sometimes it involves some tough choices. But always focus.

But what do you want more? What is a higher priority?

I would love the latest model computer and a new car, but my data says, it's not time for either. Financing a new car will create more financial stress, right now.

Importantly, wealth coach, Ann Wilson, says you should have dreams and set goals that are bigger than paying the rent.

Sarano Kelley in *The Game* says setting clear goals and targets will transform your relationship with money. Setting goals is about deciding what kind of life you want to live. What sort of lifestyle you want?

So what sort of lifestyle do you want? You have to imagine it in detail.

My friend Jake makes a very good point. "When my wife and I first got married we did not have a lot of money. We used to play 'Let's pretend' where we would imagine the sort of home we wanted to live in. The sort of car we wanted. The holidays we would go on. Things like that. A lot of those dreams came true."

This book is about taking small steps in the right direction and there is solid research that says having clear targets leads to long-term success.

Your turn

- You've read this far – what are some obvious
  financial goals (or targets)?
- What have you already identified as 'needs
  attention' or 'needs sorting'?
- What's an obvious financial target you'd like to
  work on within the next 90 days?
- If you have racked up credit card debt what plan
  could you come up with to reduce or eliminate
  that debt within the next 90 days?

Skill #3 Reducing your spending

You've probably worked it out. *Monitoring, focusing* and *reducing* go together.

Reducing is the skill you need to acquire in order to reduce debts and live on less than you earn. The first goal might be to learn to live on less than 70% of your take-home, after-tax pay.

Just about every wealth book says save 10% of your take-home, after-tax pay, use 20% to reduce your debts, and learn to live on the remaining 70% of your income.

If I make a $1 after-tax, 10c gets saved, 20c goes towards reducing debts and we live on 70c. Apply that to your weekly salary and you can see how effective this is as a money managing strategy.

There are several debt reduction strategies that work such as accelerated debt payments and debt eliminator programmes that get you to list all your debts and repayments and eliminate the smallest debts first. But these strategies don't work unless you cut spending.

Use the information you gathered in the *Monitoring* stage along with the goals you identified in the *Focusing* stage to cut spending in the *Reducing* stage.

Are you starting to get a sense of how it is so easy to spend more than you earn? Most people spend 130% of their weekly income. This means they live beyond their means and have chronic money worries.

Reducing is the skill of cutting back your spending. You will not manage your money effectively until you learn to cut your spending.

This doesn't mean becoming excessively frugal. I am talking about reducing spending on things that are a complete waste of money such as exceeding your mobile phone plan to stream games or movies.

In the last chapter I gave two examples of people that went to extreme measures to get out of debt.

Most people don't have that level of resolve or discipline to go even one week let alone 22 months.

But they did not go it alone. They sought help and support from suppliers, banks, customers, bosses, family and friends.

Reducing and monitoring go hand-in-hand. You need the data. There is no way around it. You need to know *exactly* what's happening with your spending so you know where to trim.

Whenever I talk about *reducing* people imagine they will sacrifice their nice lifestyle. Honestly, if you are in debt you don't have the lifestyle you imagine you have.

The guy that borrows from his sister knows deep down that his lifestyle is being funding by someone else's efforts. There is not accountability there. He even resents the fact he needs his sister's help! That isn't an enviable lifestyle.

These 10 principles are a reality check but if you don't have some ownership over managing your money ultimately you are wasting your time reading this book.

Reducing means changing your habits.

Remember how Diana Mathew said, "Let's *not* do lunch"? How Steven said, 'No' to his drinking buddies and Melanie said 'No' to clothes shopping?

This might mean saying 'No' to lending money to family and friends, too. Be clear if your family or friends borrowed money from a bank they would be charged the principle and interest.

Rarely do family and friends repay money they have 'borrowed'. So stop lending money. You are not a bank, an ATM machine or a registered charity.

Remember the old saying, "Giving is good as long as it doesn't hurt the giver."

Reducing requires you to clearly identify where you need to cut back. Start with whatever seems obvious to you right now like socialising, clothes shopping, doing lunch. You may also need to trim some not so obvious habits like cancelling an unused gym membership.

Get the information. It might take several months to get a clear picture because some expenses only occur on a periodic basis. But this is why you collect receipts and read bank statements.

Once Emily started collecting receipts and adding them up she discovered she was spending £1,200 a month on doing coffee and lunch. It became a lot easier to say 'No' once she realised saying 'Yes' was so expensive.

I was concerned about the high cost of our energy bills. My energy provider installed new meters along with a device that shows real-time energy consumption. We have become a lot more conscious of energy use on because we have the information.

One couple reduced their winter energy bills through installing roofing insulation, by closing doors and by turning off the radiators in unused rooms.

Cost reduction expert, Nigel Ward wrote a practical book called *Using Less Stuff!* (see Amazon) to help business owners save money on everything from utilities to energy consumption. But Nigel says these principles are easily applied to *any household*.

"Turn your central heating down one or two degrees. You will be just as comfortable at 18 as you are at 20 but your energy bills will be significantly less."

"Switch to LED light globes. Air your laundry rather than using the tumble drier. Monitor how you use anything that draws power."

"Importantly, monitor your bills and switch suppliers if you have to. Anyone can renegotiate a better tariff. Why would you want to give good money away to a energy company!"

"These are simple things anyone can do to cut costs."

Nigel says to ask for a regular review of your bills especially if you pay via direct debit. Last year we had a warm Spring and a long Summer so while we weren't using the heating our energy provider was still deducting the same rate that was then held in credit.

Check if you are eligible for a refund. That's money that should be in your bank, not theirs! Our refund paid nearly half of our Christmas gifts last year.

I gave an example earlier of a company that shaved 5% saving off their top five bills and saved £45,000 just by asking. You can do that, too.

If you own a car you are most likely wasting money by accelerating, speeding and sudden braking. David Wilson is a fuel consultant who helps his clients achieve average fuel savings of 14% by simply training drivers to slow down as they approach and then leave intersections and traffic lights. His clients typically spend £22m pa on fuel so a 14% saving of £3.08m is significant. That's the cost of several new lorries.

But he says those savings can apply to *any* motorist. His message is: *Slow down and save*. The knock-on benefit is, of course, reduced service and maintenance fees.

Wealth Chef, Ann Wilson says, "Controlling your finances is about transforming your future." And the trick to transforming your finances is accurate data.

Your turn

- Where do you obviously need to cut spending in the next 90 days?
- What needs eliminating all together?
- Get a list of all your bills and check if any of those could be renegotiated. As an exercise call one of your suppliers and tell them you'd like to find ways to reduce your energy bill. Check if they can offer you a better rate or tariff?
- What things do you buy right now that you know you actually don't need?
- Make sure you get receipts for everything and read your bank statements.

Skill #4 Developing your financial smarts

I hope by now you are forming the picture that reversing your money woes and taking charge requires information. But it also requires you to invest in your own financial education and develop your skills by applying what you are learning.

You will never wake up one morning knowing how to spend less money on things like your electricity bill let alone invest in an ISA, real estate or shares unless you start honing your financial literacy.

People who are good with their money at some point started searching the internet, reading books and magazine articles, attending short courses or seeking advice. You need to set aside time to educate yourself about how money works.

Steve Bolton runs a UK-based company called *Platinum Property Partners* that teaches people how to build wealth and achieve financial freedom through investing in property.

Steve says, "Ongoing personal and professional development will make the biggest difference to the level of success and financial freedom you achieve. Don't make the mistake of *not* investing time and money in your personal and professional development. Without a doubt it starts with learning how to manage your money."

Whatever you can do to improve your knowledge of finances, do it. Even if that starts with reading books on making or saving money.

An obvious place to start is in your local library in the *Finance* section. Start with any books on *Saving Money* or *Debt Reduction*. I've given a snapshot of some of the best money managing tips I found in books located at my local library.

Most books will cover aspects of earning, spending, saving, investing and giving. And some books will cover monitoring, targeting, reducing, developing skills and taking action.

Just make sure the books you choose are current. Have you ever been into a library and seen the software guides? You are not going to borrow a book on *Excel 2000*, right? No, it's out of date. It's the same with money books. Check the publication date.

That said, some books offer timeless advice. I read a book on how to save money on weekly shopping that was written in 1934 during the Depression that is as relevant today as it was then. It reported: 'We throw away 60% of purchased fresh produce.' That has not changed in almost 90 years.

I'm not suggesting you eat stale food.

Rather be careful when supermarket shopping to buy the right quantities of fresh produce you need for a week.

I would encourage you to read Adam Smith's *The Wealth of Nations*. But be warned, initially, this is a hard read because it is over 200 years old. But I am still amazed at how relevant this book is to anyone who wants to understand money and wealth.

Written in 1776, this book has shaped and dominated the economics of the world and once you get into it, you will find it hard to put down. You can download Smith's book for free.

But let's go with something more current.

Another obvious place to start money management training is at your bank's website. Most banks offer reliable free information, tips, tutorials and tools on managing money. And a range of online and downloadable tools like spreadsheets and budgeting Apps.

The secret is to do a little bit every day.

Most people have no idea how much good information and personal advice is offered by their bank for free. Bank staff can also refer you to qualified experts who can help you with budgeting, planning, savings, loans, insurance and so on. Start by logging on to your bank's website or visit your nearest branch.

Steve Bolton also emphasises the benefits of getting professional advice, coaching and mentoring.

Your accountant offers a lot more than simply filing your *Self Assessment* each year. They can offer practical advice and support such as bookkeeping, tax advice, budgeting and forecasting.

Financial advisors can help build a personal action plan suited to your needs and goals. And they can provide ongoing support. Ken and Peter are two experienced financial advisors based in Wales who specialise in ensuring their clients plan and fund their future - sooner.

"A lot of young people are leaving university and earning good starting salaries. One of our clients is a 24 year old programmer who earns £140,000 a year! He has been smart enough to seek investment advice but most young people will simply spend their money and end up with little to show for their efforts."

No one can help you if you don't know what money you earn, spend or save or if you have no goals or plans.

Wealth coach, Simon Jeffries also mentors some younger clients earning good money.

"The ones who get ahead think about their future and start *planning* sooner. It's amazing how quickly you can get ahead financially with the right plan."

He observes that those who struggle and end up with little to show for their efforts usually can't be bothered planning. Or even investing in knowledge and skills.

"Most people are reluctant to borrow a *free* book from a library let alone pay for a training course or work with a mentor that can help them become debt-free, financially-free or even wealthy."

Think what it would mean to be wealthy. Think about all the benefits of being in charge of your money. Then think about all the negative consequences of *not* changing your habits, beliefs, behaviours and learning new skills.

You can be debt-free within the next three to six months if you make it a priority. But you'll need to learn new ways of thinking and some new money managing skills.

The key is to start with the obvious. If the most obvious thing is to reduce your credit card bills, search the web for tips on reducing credit card bills.

The most common advice is to start reading. Old or new books, start somewhere. You will find a lot of information repeats and there is also conflicting advice but keep reading.

I read over 143 books in order to write *The Money Chimp* and most of the best money managing advice was identified in about the first 12 books. But I still kept reading picking up good ideas here and there.

Reading helps but in the end it must result in action. You must clearly identify how much money you earn, how much you spend and what you spend your money on each month and each year.

You need that information to help you decide what action is required.

Your Money Managing Profile

One of the best ways to invest in yourself is to take the online *Money Chimp* test to identify your current money managing profile. People who do *The Money Chimp* test say it was a game changer.

You answer 35 questions and instantly receive a comprehensive report. The report covers each of the 10 money managing habits *Earn, Spend, Save, Invest, Give*; and the skills of *Monitor, Focus, Reduce, Develop* and *Action*.

You also get an *Overall Score* and a graph of your individual results like the one below.

On the left hand side you can see a scale ranging 0-100%. There is also a horizontal grey zone set at the 75% mark and some vertical bars ranging in different heights.

Ideally those vertical bars need to be somewhere *inside* that grey zone. If they are *outside* the horizontal grey zone - *too high or too low* - it means it's an area requiring your attention.

The report then gives detailed feedback for each of the 10 money managing habits and skills.

The graph suggests this person doesn't earn enough, they spend too much and don't save. And they need to pick up skills in monitoring their finances. It appears this person may already be working on reducing their spending because it is in range.

In addition to the graph you also get detailed feedback on how you answered *every question*. That adds up to a clear and personalised report on your money-managing skills.

People who take *The Money Chimp* test say:

- "Really, really useful information."
- "I knew a lot of this. It was scary but also good to see what I knew confirmed in black and white."
- "This has been such a useful tool. I wish I knew this stuff years ago."
- "This test provides meaningful and relevant information with helpful suggestions."

You can take the Money Chimp test at:

www.moneychimp.net

In addition to the test read books or do courses that help you explore your beliefs and behaviours around money. I have already recommended *The Energy of Money*. You will find this challenging because it will delve into your relationship with money starting from childhood. And who has time for that, right? But you need to make time to understand how you are wired up around personal finances otherwise history will repeat itself.

The big take-away from this chapter should be: *Educate yourself about money.*

Your turn

- Do you belong to a library? Visit your local library and dig around the money section. See what books interest you.
- Borrow one book on debt reduction or saving money.

- Check the reading section in this book for a list of books I recommend.
- Google search the top 10 money saving websites.
- Have a look at the personal finance books on Amazon. There are lots! Here's a tip about Amazon. They sell both new and used copies. I recently found a great money book that was £26 new but only 40p used. Buy the used copies. I don't want you to go broke buying books on how to avoid going broke!

Skill #5 Taking Action

Let me emphasise that the ideas in this book are totally worthless if you don't take any action. Good intentions and words *without actions* are meaningless.

There is no point knowing something if you don't apply it. *To know and not to do is still not to know.* You may need to re-read that last sentence!

This report may be interesting but useless if you don't take action.

You have to start somewhere. Think of it this way, you are not a victim to money. Money does not control you. Money is inanimate, lifeless. Your habits and choices and skills and attitude are the deciding factors.

I've given many examples and in each case the ability to manage money improved dramatically by trying the ideas and giving them a fair go.

In some cases, you'll need to develop new habits.

Most money managing books and courses say you have to spend less than you earn. That makes total sense, right?

They all suggest to pay yourself first or try and save 10% of your after-tax, take-home pay.

They all suggest you set money aside for emergencies. Some suggest you get ahead by learning to live on less than 70% of your after-tax, take-home pay. We know that it's achievable and in most cases people can get their finances under control within 90 days and even be debt free but none of that will happen until you take action.

If you fail to action you need to ask yourself why. Why exactly are you exempt from being responsible with money? What's going on?

You may have to collect receipts for at least three months before a clear picture emerges. I know most people will lose interest after a week. You have to push through that. You might have to start monitoring more closely. But if you stick to it results come very fast. You may have to trim back gently or drastically.

It might be embarrassing to ask for a receipt but that little piece of paper might be an important piece to your money puzzle if a pattern starts to emerge.

Humans behave in predictable ways. We stick with familiar habits even if those habits are detrimental!

Take smoking or drinking. Remember Luke? He drinks and smokes to feel accepted by his mates at the pub. Those mates buy each other drinks and share cigarettes but who gets rich and who pays? When Luke thought about it he realised he was not really into football and he hated wasting his weekends at the pub watching football. When he looked back he realised he pretty much arrived at the bar on a Friday night and didn't go home until Sunday afternoon. For five years!

You may have to set some targets. It's not easy negotiating a new phone rate or gas bill or swapping energy providers. You can easily spend 20 minutes on hold. It's not easy moving house when you know you are paying £800 PCM more than you need to for the convenience of living 10 minutes closer to work.

You might need to trim your spending starting with eliminating items you don't really need to buy. You don't need new shoes each month. Or a *PlayStation*. Or an *iWatch* on a payment plan. You don't need to spend £180 per week on alcohol.

You might need to make a huge effort to reduce your credit card debts. You might need to take a second job just to pay off your credit card.

You might need to get uncomfortable and take on some accountability around managing money.

You might need to learn *impulse control* and *delayed gratification*. Most human problems come down to those two issues – the inability to resist impulses and delay gratification.

The fact that you are sitting there and not peeing your

pants right now comes down to the ability to control urges and impulses. As an adult you must learn to control the impulse to spend £400 a month on clothes to bolster your self-esteem and win approval.

I recently listened to a CD on *mindfulness*. One section covered coping with *urges*. Most urges really only last about 10 minutes and then pass. If you have the urge to buy new shoes, go breathe instead! Focus on your in-breath and out-breath. If your mind wanders back to buying shoes just go back to focusing on your in- and out-breath.

You might need to learn to say 'No' to others – maybe family members or even yourself.

Delayed gratification means postponing rewards to the future such as saving money for a holiday, a car or a house deposit. Basically you sacrifice the immediate gratification you get from spending right now.

Every book I reviewed says save money and then invest. You cannot do the most basic investment strategies without some money behind you.

I think profiling your money managing habits is a great investment in your future. I created *The Money Chimp* test to help you better understand your relationship with money and your current skills and habits.

People in the UK, USA and Australia say that the test is accurate and has been incredibly helpful.

Reading books is an investment in your financial literacy.

So what if you find the book boring? Try another one. As I've said every book says *none* of these ideas work unless you take action – preferably today!

Taking action is hard. It can feel like trying to roll a car out of the mud. It seems like you're getting nowhere at first. But persist. Managing your money wisely is possibly one of the most important, lifelong skills you will ever master.

Every book I read suggests seeking good advice. There are free and inexpensive advisory services and high end advisors like Ken and Peter. You would be silly to doubt the need for financial advice.

Your local bank has an excellent free service for anyone who needs to set up a household budget and special banking services such as a target account.

You can read books and do training courses on property investing. Doing the *Money Chimp* workshop or spending a day with someone like Steve Bolton will give you much more than just good information.

Many training programmes include a community of like-minded people and a level of support you cannot get from a book. Sometimes the insight comes through conversations and asking questions.

You might even benefit by re-reading this book several times.

Your turn

- If you got this far you will definitely have some ideas to put into action. Write a list of obvious action steps and pick three – one hard and two easy - and get cracking.
- There are plenty of examples in this book of people who took simple actions and achieved great results. Remember the university students who cleared their credit card debt within three months? Which examples resonate with you most?
- Revisit the section on STOP, START and CONTINUE.

The Bonus Principle

There is a bonus principle hidden in these pages. You may need to re-read this book to find it but I guarantee it will jump out at you.

If you want to be a champ, re-read this book anyway because I know you will have missed a nugget.

That bonus principle is like a key. It will turbo charge your motivation to manage your money effectively. It may inspire you to become debt-free and even financially-free for life.

One reader said that the bonus principle that jumped out at him was 'Get good advice'. It wasn't the one I deliberately buried but that's still pretty good!

So re-read each chapter and I guarantee you will experience a personally relevant light bulb moment that will change your life.

Part 5

What to do if you are in debt

Do you have a debt problem?

Money worries live on a spectrum from none, mild, and moderate to serious and extreme. Which one sounds like you?

Any money worry can be frustrating or stressful even frightening but what's important is the perception of your own ability to sort them out.

If you know you have credit card debt but believe you could get your credit card debt under control easily, then yes, it's a money worry, but it's mild. However if the repossessors are banging at the door, you're worried sick and you can't sleep at night then it's serious and you should seek help today!

This book was designed to give practical help. Sometimes distress over money is extreme. Sadly, a friend of mine committed suicide because his bills got out of control. Don't panic and don't isolate yourself. *No matter how hopeless things might seem and how despairing you feel* remember help is available.

To be clear, *The Money Chimp* is intended for people with mild to moderate money worries. In all cases you should feel you can take positive actions today and start seeing results quickly. If you are like most people you will start to see positive results within the next 90 days if you start applying some of the recommendations in this book.

For people who complete the *The Money Chimp* questionnaire and recognise serious and extreme debt problems seek professional help from a qualified financial advisor.

Even serious money worries can be turned around.

The Money Chimp test will give you a clear heads-up on your habits and skills and sometimes that's all that's needed to inspire you to take charge. Take the quick test at *www.moneychimp.net*

If you aren't sure if you need to take *The Money Chimp* test then highlight the questions that apply to you:

- Do you usually run out of spending money before the end of the week?
- Do you often get bills you can't pay on time?
- Have you got more than two credit cards with constantly rising balances, fees and interest payments?
- Do you pay just the minimum amount off each card each month?
- Have you run up debts on store cards?
- Have you got loans?
- Do you miss loan repayments?
- Do you borrow to pay off your debts?

- Do you have trouble paying for the essentials - mortgage/rent, food, gas, electricity, phone etc?
- Do you regularly pay for basic living expenses such as groceries on your credit card because you have no cash?
- Do you receive 'disconnection' warning letters from suppliers or threatening 'demand' letters from debt collectors?
- Do you regularly borrow money from family or friends and hardly ever repay it?
- Do you resent people who have money?
- Do you think about winning the lottery as the solution to your money worries?
- Do you argue with your partner over money?

If you said YES to more than three of these questions you could have a debt problem. If so, you need to get advice about managing your money immediately. And you need to make reducing and clearing your debts a priority.

However there's a lot you can do right now that will steer you towards being debt-free.

Visit your local library

As mentioned most libraries have a vast selection of books and DVDs on money that cover the topics of *Earning, Spending, Saving, Investing* and *Giving* and the skills of *Monitoring, Focusing, Reducing, Developing* and *Taking Action*.

And better still everything is free or low cost.

I read over 143 books on managing personal finances and the full range of the five topics are fully covered in libraries!

Search the Internet

While there is also an abundance of information on the Internet be careful. Make sure that it is current and relevant to *your* situation. Stay away from paid sites for now. Do not supply your credit card details to any online programmes no matter how enticing. Some unscrupulous sites can start deducting regular payments without you realising!

Seek help from professionals

If you are experiencing debt problems talk to a financial advisor or an accountant. Start with your bank and any of the government agencies that offer free or low-cost advice and support.

Rely on family or friends for support, not advice

Family members and friends are usually good for emotional support but are not typically a reliable source of advice especially if they are financially struggling themselves. They are well-intended but often misinformed and not up-to-date on current financial information. Again, seek professional advice.

DIY courses

There are many self-help courses. Understand that if you do nothing else but learn how to closely monitor what you spend for the next 90 days you will start to improve your ability to manage your money.

Attend a scheduled workshop/course

Money Chimp offers workshops on managing personal finances but there are lots of free or low cost courses on offer close to where you live.

The *Citizens Advice Bureaux* can steer you towards reputable courses. Contact them at:

www.citizensadvice.org.uk
www.debt-help-pros.com/citizensadvice.php

Tell the truth about what's happening

Far too often I meet with people who are in trouble financially and they haven't shared that information with the people who matter most. I recently chatted with a 30 year-old who was maxed out on his credit card and thousands of pounds in debt and hadn't told his girlfriend because he didn't want her to worry.

As hard as it might be, you may need to start by being honest about what's happening.

Managing your money is actually a lifelong skill and fortunately most people can start to improve their financial situation within 90 days.

This book gives you some of the tools to get going.

If you need to be debt-free

Some people are a little in debt and some are deeply in debt. Irrespective of the size, if you have any debt problems, you need to take immediate action to control your debts over the next 90 days.

Here's what works consistently:

Gather up *every* money-related bill, statement and letter you can find and collate them neatly in one folder

Look for everything to do with your money such as bills, statements and receipts.

Sort them into categories

- Credit card statements
- Bank statements
- Charge card statements
- Loans statements
- Bills
- Debt repayment letters/demand notices

Get a complete list of every debt you owe with the amount plus the fees, charges and interest owed

Top priority debts are:

- Mortgage/rent
- Loans such as student loans, housing loans
- Tax etc (HMRC, VAT etc)
- Council rates
- Utilities bills
- Licenses and registrations, TV, car etc.

These creditors *can and will* take strong legal action against you.

Low priority debts are:

- Credit cards and charge cards
- Unsecured loans such as finance loans
- Overdrafts
- Store card purchases such as furniture
- Borrowings from family or friends

Warning: These creditors are less pressing but you can still end up in court and hit with the debts plus interest *and high legal costs.*

Only seek help from qualified advisors

Start with the *Citizens Advice Bureaux.* Ultimately the key is to create a reduction plan that suits your circumstances. Once you have that plan contact everyone you owe money to and keep them informed. And then stick to the plan. Do not ignore your creditors.

Avoid High Street short-term money lenders. These high interest loans are dangerous because they typically start a new cycle of debt that worsens your situation.

If you are in financial trouble

Your number one goal is to get out of financial trouble! Once debt-free, you can start fresh with the principle of spending less than what you earn.

Credit and store card debts are crushing. Credit cards make it very easy to have what you want instantly! But this is a serious mistake if you cannot manage your money.

But the real problem is giving into negativity and a lack of self-discipline.

As I've said the fastest escape route from financial woes is to save 10% no matter what, try to reduce your debts with 20% of your income and learn to live on 70% of your take-home pay.

If you are in serious financial trouble please contact:

www.citizensadvice.org.uk

In most cases they can *quickly* assess your needs, devise a debt-reduction plan, point you in the right direction and support you in becoming debt-free.

Do not ever be tempted to do anything illegal

Countless people make life worse by trying to solve financial difficulties by doing something illegal. Even starting a cash-only business like ironing or house cleaning will get you into trouble if you don't declare your earnings.

Don't do anything stupid or desperate

Recently there was a $303 million lottery jackpot in America. I read about a young man - deeply in debt - who took his life savings *and* borrowed thousands to buy hundreds of lottery tickets. *None of them won.*

I recently heard of a guy who transferred all his life savings to a 'lawyer' in Nigeria who said a relative had died and left him $14 million in cash and all he needed to do was to transfer $15,000 to process the stamp duty. Of course this was a blatant scam.

Sadly, there are ruthless people who prey on the vulnerable. If you are in debt you are not thinking clearly and more susceptible to scams.

Don't do anything expensive

There are people who claim they can help you for an exorbitant fee. But don't get conned into paying huge fees for general advice that is freely available.

Yes, the *Money Chimp* test has a small price tag but it's cheaper than a pub meal, or a cappuccino and cake with a friend and has game changing value.

Start where you are right now

Remember Jake? He started cleaning the windows and front yards of homes in his street. Most of his clients lived within half a mile of his home and pretty soon he was earning $15 per hour, six hours a day, five days a week. Potentially, that's $450 a week!

Did he want to be a cleaner? No, he is saving up to buy camera equipment because he wants to be a portrait photographer. But for now, he is a cleaner. And with his determination he will get there.

Tell the truth

If you are debt tell the truth to the people who matter most to you. Most people *can* handle the truth. What they can't handle is discovering you've known the truth for a long time and didn't tell them.

Telling the truth starts by gathering the facts so you can give an accurate picture.

Solving your money worries will take time, smart thinking and hard work. It may not be easy, but everyone who dug themselves out from under a mountain of debt applied the strategies in this book.

If all you can do right now is borrow a book from the library or visit a debt reduction or money managing website, then start there.

Will you learn to manage you money and *stay out of debt?*

Let me repeat the good news. You can learn to manage your money and be debt-free within 90 days. But will you *stay* out of debt?

Wealth coach, Karen Sutton-Johal understands chronic debt better than most. She grew up in a family that experienced a continuous cycle of crippling debt. But she learned how to exit that cycle - *and stay out of debt* - and now teaches others how to do the same.

She has an interesting observation: "I specialise in helping people get debt-free by applying some practical tools and skills.

"But I noticed that my clients often *went straight back to being in debt again.* I realised that what needs to change is your mind-set. You really do have to think differently about money if you are in debt. I honestly believe it's because you have a *debt mind-set.*"

Karen has identified four money mind-sets:

- Debt
- Break-even
- Comfortable and
- Rich (financially free)

Having helped thousands of clients get out of debt and stay out of debt, she says the key to staying debt-free is shifting your mind-set.

"I can get you out of debt but unless you change your mind-set and relationship with money you will most likely be back in debt sooner or later, and usually sooner. But in most cases you will make the problem worse."

Changing your mind-set starts with deciding to manage your money better. You can make the life changing decision to be debt-free and financially free. Start thinking and acting differently in your attitudes to money.

You might need help from a wealth coach or a financial advisor. Investing in your financial education is worthwhile. Start the process by reading books.

A final word on credit cards

Do you have a credit card? Do you always pay off the outstanding balance by the end of the month? If so, well done! You are an exception to the rule and a money champ!

I have encouraged you to reduce or eliminate credit card debt because it is the number one problem for young adults.

Banks and credit card companies profit from interest fees and charges from people who cannot pay off the outstanding monthly balance.

Debt charities like *StepChange*, exist to offer free advice and solutions for people struggling with debt problems. *StepChange* estimate that the majority of their clients suffer from credit card debt and the average debt exceeds £8,000.

StepChange reported that over 14 million people in 2015 experienced *income shock* through changing circumstances. Over four million relied on credit to cover basic necessities. And people who rely on their credit card to cope are 20 times more likely to enter a long-term crippling debt cycle.

According to the *Financial Conduct Authority*, credit card debt in 2015 was around £61 billion with a disturbing number of consumers in arrears or defaulting.

They suggest that too many credit card users only manage to make minimum monthly repayments to cover interest. If this sounds like you then you can easily find yourself paying off a credit card balance for years.

Understand it is not the job of a credit card company to manage your money. That is your job.

Credit card debt is insidious and if you have an outstanding balance that isn't reducing you should make this a focus of action.

I have given several inspiring examples of young people who reduced or eliminated credit card debt. It took hard work and focused effort.

Here's a sample of websites you might explore if you have debt problems. These resources will help you with information and support.

www.moneyadviceservice.org.uk
www.adviceuk.org.uk
www.stepchange.org
www.nationaldebtline.org
www.stepchange.org
www.businessdebtline.org
www.capuk.org
www.citizensadvice.org.uk
www.debtadvicefoundation.org

Let me know how you are going

I am pleased to say the ideas in *The Money Chimp* work! But only you can prove that for yourself. I love hearing success stories and getting feedback.

I encourage you to share your journey of discovery and any testimonials because they inspire others to succeed.

Please email me at:

feedback@moneychimp.net

With your permission, I'd like to include your stories on my website at

www.moneychimp.net

I am constantly adding free downloads to ensure you stay a happy *Money Champ!*

References

- Aaron, Raymond. (2008). *Double Your Income By Doing What You Love*, Wiley.
- Bachrach, Bill. (2000). *Values Based Financial Planning*, Aim High Publishing.
- Bolton, Steve. (2012). *Successful Property Investing: How to Earn £50,000 to £150,000 in Two to Five Years*, A Platinum Partners Press Book.
- Clason, George, S. (1926). *The Richest Man in Babylon*, Hawthorn/Dutton.
- Conwell, Russell. (1915). *Acres of Diamonds.*
- Coonradt, Charles et al. (1996). *The Four Laws of Debt Free Prosperity, Chequemate International.*
- Eisenberg, Lee. (2006). *The Number*, Free Press.
- Grant, Patrick. (2015). *Planning For Retirement,* Straightforward Guides.
- Kelley, Sarano. (2001). *The Game*. Jodere Group.
- Kiyosaki, Robert. (1997). Rich Dad, Poor Dad. TechPress, Inc.
- Lewis, Martin. (2005).*The Money Diet*. Vermilion.
- Lewis, Martin. (2006). *Thrifty Ways For Modern Days.* Vermilion
- Lewis, Martin. (2008). *The Three Most Important Lessons You've Never Been Taught.* Vermilion
- Nemeth, Maria. (1997). *The Energy of Money,* Ballatine Wellspring.

- Mathew, Diana. (1996). *The Money Tree,* National Direct Marketing.
- McKinnon, Shirley. (2001). *Coach Yourself to Wealth*, Crown Content.
- Millar, Caroline Adams. (2009). *Creating Your Best Life,* Sterling.
- Nutting, John. (2015). *Growing Awareness.* Nutting.
- Prochanska, James, O. et al. (1994). *Changing for Good: A revolutionary six-stage program for overcoming bad habits and moving your life positively forward.* Collins Living.
- Richards, Carl. (2015). *The One Page Financial Plan: A simple way to be smart about your money.* Psychologies, October 2015.
- Schafer, Bodo. (1999). *The Road to Financial Freedom*, Griffin Press.
- Stanton, Dr. Harry E. (1979). *The Plus Factor,* Optima Books.
- Stanton, Dr. Harry E. (1997). *Let the Trade Winds Flow.*
- Ward, Nigel. (2013). *Using Less Stuff.* Writing Matters Publishing.
- Warner, Stuart. (2010). *Secrets Finance Basics,* Harper Collins.
- Wilson, Ann. (2014). *The Wealth Chef.* Hay House.
- Wusche, Vicki. (2010). *How to Invest in Property.* SRA Books.
- Wusche, Vicki. (2012) . *Property for the Next Generation: Preparing Your Family for a Wealthy Future.* SRA Books

About the Author

Andrew Priestley is an award winning business coach who has worked with entrepreneurs and business owners in Australia and the UK for 17 years.

He believes many business owners do not understand basic personal finances let alone business finance.

After an extensive review of money managing literature, he created the *The Money Chimp* profile to help people identify their money managing strengths and weaknesses.

He runs *The Money Chimp* workshop designed for young people aged 18-25. Participants see a significant change in their finances within 90 days.

Andrew says: "Young adults aged 18-25 typically spend 130 % of their weekly income and are the most susceptible to entering a cycle of crippling debt.

"I really hope the habits and skills in *The Money Chimp* helps you to become debt-free and sets you on the road to financial freedom."

Contact

CHUMP · · · · · CHIMP · · · · · CHAMP!

The Money Chimp Test
www.moneychimp.net

Business Finance
How Money Flows Through Your Business

Business coaching
www.andrewpriestley.com

Business development
Starting! (Amazon)

The Sales Profile
www.thesalesprofile.com